hamlyn

DENISE SMART

PRESSURE COOKING EVERY DAY

80 MODERN RECIPES FOR STOVETOP PRESSURE COOKING

An Hachette UK Company
www.hachette.co.uk

First published in Great Britain in 2019 by Hamlyn, an imprint of
Octopus Publishing Group Ltd
Carmelite House
50 Victoria Embankment
London EC4Y 0DZ
www.octopusbooks.co.uk

Distributed in the US by
Hachette Book Group
1290 Avenue of the Americas
4th and 5th Floors
New York, NY 10104

Distributed in Canada by
Canadian Manda Group
664 Annette St.
Toronto, Ontario, Canada M6S 2C8

ISBN 978-0-600-63578-9

A CIP catalogue record for this book is available from the
British Library.

Printed and bound in China

10 9 8 7 6 5 4 3 2 1

Standard level spoon measurements are used in all recipes.
1 tablespoon = one 15 ml spoon
1 teaspoon = one 5 ml spoon

Both imperial and metric measurements have been given in all recipes.
Use one set of measurements only and not a mixture of both.

Eggs should be medium, milk should be full fat and fresh herbs
should be used unless otherwise stated.

Editorial Director: Eleanor Maxfield
Junior Editor: Sarah Vaughan
Art Director: Isabel de Cordova
Designer: Megan Van Staden
Photographer: William Shaw
Food Stylist: Denise Smart
Prop Stylist: Cynthia Blackett
Assistant Production Manager: Lucy Carter

CONTENTS

INTRODUCTION

Today's stovetop pressure cookers have been redesigned with many new safety features. Gone are the days of their fearsome reputation of rattling away on the stove with the worry of exploding!

Pressure cooking has become fashionable again, with many of today's top chefs using them in their kitchens, and they are often seen on cooking shows and competitions, when time is of the essence. They are no longer just used for cooking tougher cuts of meat and beans and lentils, but are ideal for everyday cooking.

This quick way of cooking makes light work of stocks, soups, stews, pasta, rice, vegetables, fish, desserts, baking, preserves and chutneys, which you will see when you browse through the recipes.

Pressure cooking is a cooking method that uses steam sealed in the cooker, which is a special airtight cooking pot. Heating a liquid such as water, wine, stock or broth in a pressure cooker traps the vapour that rises from the liquid. This in turn can raise the temperature inside the cooker up to 121°C (250°F). The increased temperature and pressure significantly speed up the cooking as steam is forced through the food, which means that pressure cooking can cook foods in a third of the ordinary time.

The recipes in this book were all cooked in a pressure cooker with a 5–6 litre (8¾–10½ pint) capacity. This way you can cook larger quantities of food and bigger cuts of meat. Try and choose a wider model if possible, so you can fit in cake tins and ovenproof baking dishes. A wider dish also makes browning meat much easier.

All pressure cookers work on the same principle, but always read the manufacturer's instructions for your cooker, before using.

SETTING THE PRESSURE

All pressure cookers have high and low pressure settings. Choose a cooker with a PSI (pounds per square inch) of between 12–15 for high pressure and 6–8 for low pressure. The recipe will tell you which pressure to select.

STABILIZING THE PRESSURE

Once pressure has been reached the indicator will show this and the cooker will be sealed. Wait until you hear a hissing sound – this is the cue to start timing your recipe – then reduce the heat to maintain the pressure. You may want to start off over a large ring, then move to a smaller ring to maintain the pressure (a heat diffusion mat is ideal). Aim to maintain a gentle hissing sound.

RELEASING PRESSURE

There are two methods of releasing pressure: slow release, where the pressure is allowed to drop naturally, so the food will continue to cook, or quick release where the pressure is released immediately after the cooking time is complete. Most modern cookers will come with a fast release mechanism or you may have to run the cooker under cold water.

EQUIPMENT

Your pressure cooker should come with a trivet, ideal for placing large items on, and a steamer basket, which can be upturned to balance smaller items, such as ramekins, on. To make many of the recipes in the book you will also need small ramekins, ovenproof dishes and cake tins (about 18–20 cm/7–8 inches) and a selection of pudding basins. You will also need nonstick baking paper and foil. Most recipes do not need covering, as this will slow down the cooking time; however, you will need to cover steamed puddings, suet puddings and fish. A tea towel is also useful to wrap dishes in, making them easier to remove, or you can make a foil handle by folding over the foil and using to wrap under the dish.

BENEFITS OF USING A STOVETOP PRESSURE COOKER

SUPER QUICK – cooks three times faster than conventional cooking – electrical versions are, on average, only twice as fast.

CONVENIENCE – delicious, flavoursome meals using just one pot. A pressure cooker is also perfect for busy people, as you can make a nutritious, tasty midweek meal in under 20 minutes, or batch cook and freeze for later.

ECONOMICAL – pressure cookers are ideal for cooking very cheap ingredients from scratch: dried beans, pulses and cheaper cuts of meat, and as cooking times are drastically reduced they also save energy costs.

DURABILITY – electric pressure cookers will last for years; stovetop cookers will last a lifetime.

MORE POWER – stovetop pressure cookers reach higher heat and pressure than electrical versions, which is particularly good for advanced pressure cooking techniques and means quicker cooking.

RETAINS NUTRIENTS AND TASTE – with pressure cooking there is no compromise on taste and texture; in many cases, the flavours are intensified. It also retains vitamins and nutrients.

USEFUL HINTS AND TIPS

- Use a timer as cooking times can be short. The difference between a minute or two can result in a perfect or spoiled dish.

- Do not overfill.

- Thicken stews at the end of the cooking time.

- Always add the minimum amount of liquid recommended by the manufacturer.

- Never leave the pressure cooker unattended.

- Always release pressure away from you.

- Do not add milk or cream to your sauces until the end as they will curdle. (Except in puddings, which are cooked at low pressure.)

- Use liquids that produce steam, such as water, stock and wine (never oil!).

- Add a tablespoon of oil and a pinch of salt to lentils and beans when cooking as this prevent them frothing up.

- Never force the lid of a pressure cooker open.

This book contains a great mix of easy-to-follow recipes, from familiar dishes to more adventurous recipes from around the world as well as ones you never thought were possible in a pressure cooker. You will find modern recipes for meat-eaters and vegetarians as well as for every meal occasion, whether it is informal entertaining, midweek meals, lighter bites or even date night!

Like me, I hope you will find a new enthusiasm for your pressure cooker and will be encouraged to use yours more.

BRUNCH AND LUNCH

SERVES: 2
Preparation time: 5 minutes
Cooking time: 12 minutes (Low pressure)

QUINOA, SMOKED HADDOCK AND SPINACH KEDGEREE

1 tablespoon sunflower oil
knob of butter
1 red onion, sliced
1 teaspoon grated fresh root ginger
150 g (5 oz) quinoa, rinsed
2 teaspoons curry powder
300 ml (½ pint) hot fish or vegetable
    stock
2 skinless smoked haddock loins,
    about 125 g (4 oz) each
2 eggs
50 g (2 oz) baby spinach
juice of 1 large lemon
salt and freshly ground black pepper

You can cook boiled eggs in the pressure cooker under low pressure – they are so easy to peel.

Heat the oil and butter in the bottom of the pressure cooker, add the onion and ginger and cook over a medium heat for 2–3 minutes until softened. Stir in the quinoa and cook for 2 minutes until lightly toasted, then add the curry powder, season with salt and pepper and stir to coat the quinoa. Leave to stand for 2–3 minutes so the quinoa becomes tender.

Pour over the hot stock and bring to a simmer, then place the haddock on top. Place the eggs in the steamer basket and place in the cooker. Lock the lid, bring up to low pressure, stabilize the heat and cook for 6 minutes. Remove from the heat and quick release. Plunge the eggs into cold water.

Stir the quinoa to break the fish into large flakes, then stir in the spinach to wilt. Half-cover with the lid and leave to stand for 2–3 minutes while you peel the eggs.

Stir the lemon juice into the quinoa, then divide between 2 bowls. Halve the eggs and serve on top with freshly ground black pepper and lemon wedges, to garnish.

SERVES: 4—6
Preparation time: 5 minutes, plus soaking overnight
Cooking time: 20 minutes (High pressure)

CREAMY HUMMUS

150 g (5 oz) dried chickpeas, soaked overnight
3 tablespoons olive oil, plus extra to serve
4 tablespoons well-stirred tahini
juice of 1 large lemon
1 small garlic clove, crushed
½ teaspoon ground cumin
½ teaspoon salt
salt and freshly ground black pepper
pinch of ground paprika, to garnish

To serve:
warmed pitta breads
vegetable crudités

Drain and rinse the chickpeas and place them in the pressure cooker. Cover with water up to halfway, then add 1 tablespoon of the oil and half the salt. Lock the lid, bring up to high pressure, stabilize the heat and cook for 20 minutes. Remove from the heat and slow release. Drain the chickpeas, reserving 6 tablespoons of the cooking water.

Meanwhile, place the tahini and lemon juice in a food processor and process until lightly whisked, scraping the sides down with a spatula.

Add the garlic, cumin, remaining olive oil and salt to the whisked tahini and lemon juice. Process for 30 seconds, scrape the sides and bottom of the bowl, then process for another 30 seconds, or until well blended.

Add half the chickpeas and process again for about 1 minute. Scrape down the sides of the bowl, add the remaining chickpeas, then blend until smooth.

Add 3—4 tablespoons of the reserved cooking water and blend again until the hummus is smooth, adding more water if necessary. Season to taste.

Transfer the hummus to a bowl, drizzle with a little extra olive oil and sprinkle with a little paprika. Serve with warm pitta bread and vegetable crudités.

SERVES: 4
Preparation time: 10 minutes
Cooking time: 9 minutes (High pressure)

BREAKFAST HASH

2 tablespoons sunflower oil
750 g (1½ lb) potatoes, peeled and cut into small cubes
1 large onion, sliced
6 sausages, skins removed and cut into pieces
4 smoked back bacon rashers, chopped
150 ml (¼ pint) hot chicken stock
salt and freshly ground black pepper

To serve:
fried eggs
brown sauce or tomato ketchup

Heat the oil in the pressure cooker over a high heat, add the potatoes, onion, sausages and bacon and cook for 3–4 minutes, stirring occasionally, until the potatoes and sausages are lightly browned.

Pour over the hot stock and season well. Lock the lid, bring up to high pressure, stabilize the heat and cook for 5 minutes. Remove from the heat and quick release.

Divide among 4 plates and serve each topped with a fried egg and brown sauce or ketchup.

SERVES: 4
Preparation time: 10 minutes
Cooking time: 9 minutes (High pressure)

CAPONATA

2 aubergines, cut into 3.5 cm
(1½ inch) pieces
2 tablespoons olive oil
1 large red onion, sliced
1 celery stick, cut into 2.5 cm (1 inch)
pieces
150 g (5 oz) ripe tomatoes, diced
100 ml (3½ fl oz) tomato passata
1 tablespoon tomato purée
2 tablespoons red wine vinegar
1 tablespoon caster sugar
2 tablespoons chopped green olives
1 tablespoon capers, rinsed
2 tablespoons sultanas or raisins
2 tablespoons toasted pine nuts
small bunch of basil, shredded
salt and freshly ground black pepper

To serve:
toasted sourdough
mozzarella cheese or prosciutto

This Sicilian aubergine stew is delicious served warm or cold on toasted sourdough with mozzarella or prosciutto. This stew tastes even better the next day.

Place the aubergines in a bowl of cold water for 5 minutes (this stops them absorbing too much oil), then drain and pat dry with kitchen paper.

Heat the oil in the pressure cooker over a medium heat, add the onion, celery and aubergines and cook for 4 minutes until soft and beginning to colour. Stir in the diced tomatoes, passata, tomato purée, vinegar and sugar. Stir to coat, then add the olives, capers and sultanas or raisins. Season with a little salt and pepper.

Lock the lid, bring up to high pressure, stabilize the heat and cook for 4 minutes. Remove from the heat and quick release.

Leave to cool slightly, then stir in the pine nuts. Stir in the basil just before serving on toasted sourdough with mozzarella or prosciutto.

SERVES: 4
Preparation time: 10 minutes
Cooking time: 6 minutes (High pressure)

WARM BEETROOT, LENTIL AND GOATS' CHEESE SALAD

200 g (7 oz) dried green lentils, rinsed

3 tablespoons walnut oil

½ teaspoon salt

300 ml (½ pint) hot vegetable stock

4 small fresh beetroot, each peeled and cut into 6 thin wedges

125 g (4 oz) roasted red peppers in brine or oil, drained and chopped

50 g (1 oz) walnut pieces

125 g (4 oz) baby spinach

125 g (4 oz) goats' cheese log, crumbled or roughly sliced

For the dressing:

2 tablespoons balsamic vinegar

1 teaspoon Dijon mustard

salt and freshly ground black pepper

Place the lentils, 1 tablespoon of the walnut oil and the salt in the pressure cooker, then pour over the hot stock. Place the steamer basket in the cooker and add the beetroot. Lock the lid, bring up to high pressure, stabilize the heat and cook for 6 minutes. Remove from the heat and slow release. Check the lentils are tender and simmer for a few more minutes if necessary.

Meanwhile, whisk together the remaining walnut oil with the dressing ingredients in a small bowl. Set aside.

Drain the lentils, place in a bowl with the beetroot wedges and pour over two-thirds of the dressing. Add the red peppers and walnuts and mix gently to combine.

Divide the spinach between 4 plates and add the lentil mixture, then crumble over the goats' cheese. Drizzle over the remaining dressing and serve immediately.

SERVES: 4
Preparation time: 10 minutes
Cooking time: about 8 minutes (High pressure)

SCANDI POTATO AND SMOKED MACKEREL SALAD

1 red onion, finely sliced
1 tablespoon red wine vinegar
1 tablespoon olive oil
15 g (½ oz) unsalted butter
500 g (1 lb) new potatoes, halved if large
4 tablespoons water
50 g (2 oz) soured cream or crème fraîche
50 g (2 oz) light mayonnaise
small bunch of dill, roughly chopped
small bunch of parsley, roughly chopped
1 tablespoon capers, rinsed and chopped
50 g (2 oz) radishes, sliced
4 peppered smoked mackerel fillets, skin removed and flaked
salt and freshly ground black pepper

Mix the onion and vinegar together in a small bowl, then set aside while you cook the potatoes.

Heat the oil and butter in the pressure cooker over a high heat, add the potatoes and fry for about 3 minutes, or until starting to brown. Add the measured water and season with salt and pepper. Lock the lid, bring up to high pressure, stabilize the heat and cook for 5 minutes. Remove from the heat and slow release. Drain the potatoes, place in a serving dish and leave to cool slightly.

Mix the soured cream or crème fraîche, mayonnaise, herbs and capers together in a bowl. Stir into the potatoes and season to taste.

Drain the pickled onions (from step 1) of any excess vinegar, then stir through the potato salad.

Arrange on a platter, then scatter over the radishes and mackerel. Serve immediately.

SERVES: 4
Preparation time: 10 minutes
Cooking time: 10 minutes (High pressure)

CARIBBEAN BUTTERNUT SQUASH SOUP

1 tablespoon olive oil
1 large onion, sliced
1 tablespoon grated fresh root ginger
1 potato, about 250 g (8 oz), peeled and
    chopped
500 g (1 lb) peeled butternut squash,
    cut into 1.5 cm (¾ inch) cubes
1 red pepper, cored, deseeded and
    chopped
2 teaspoons jerk seasoning
600 ml (1 pint) hot chicken or
    vegetable stock
300 ml (½ pint) coconut milk
juice of 1 lime
salt and freshly ground black pepper

To serve:
sliced red chillies (optional)
a few sprigs of fresh coriander

Heat the oil in the pressure cooker over a medium heat, add the onion and ginger and cook for 2–3 minutes until softened, stirring occasionally. Stir in the potato, butternut squash, red pepper and jerk seasoning and cook for a further 2 minutes.

Pour in the hot stock and coconut milk and stir well. Lock the lid, bring up to high pressure, stabilize the heat and cook for 5 minutes. Remove from the heat and slow release.

Using a stick blender, blend until smooth. Alternatively, transfer to a blender or food processor and blend until smooth. Squeeze in the lime juice and season to taste. Serve in bowls garnished with sliced chillies, if using, and coriander sprigs.

SERVES: 4
Preparation time: 10 minutes
Cooking time: 12 minutes (High pressure)

PEA, MINT AND FETA FRITTITA

softened butter, for greasing
200 g (7 oz) frozen peas
150 g (5 oz) feta cheese, crumbled
pinch of dried chilli flakes
2 tablespoons chopped mint
5 eggs, beaten
freshly ground black pepper
pea shoots, to garnish

Lightly grease an 18 cm (7 inch) non stick cake tin (not loose-bottomed) and line the base with nonstick baking paper.

Put the peas in a heatproof bowl and pour over enough just-boiled water to cover. Leave for 1 minute, then drain the peas in a sieve and tip them back into the bowl. Add the feta, sprinkle over the chilli and mint and season with lots of black pepper.

Beat the eggs together in another bowl, then stir in two-thirds of the pea and mint mixture. Pour into the tin, then sprinkle over the remaining mixture.

Place the trivet or upturned steamer basket in the pressure cooker and pour in enough water to come just below the top of the trivet or basket. Carefully lower in the tin.

Lock the lid, bring up to high pressure, stabilize the heat and cook for 12 minutes. Remove from the heat and slow release. Carefully remove the frittita from the pressure cooker, transfer to a board and cut into wedges.

Serve garnished with pea shoots.

SERVES: 2
Preparation time: 8 minutes
Cooking time: 12 minutes (High pressure)

VIETNAMESE CHICKEN PHO

2 teaspoons sunflower oil
1 teaspoon black peppercorns
1 lemon grass stalk, tough outer layers
   removed and sliced
½ cinnamon stick
½ teaspoon coriander seeds
1 star anise
2.5 cm (1 inch) piece of fresh root
   ginger, peeled and thinly sliced
4 skinless, boneless chicken thighs
600 ml (1 pint) water
150 g (5 oz) dried rice stick noodles
2 teaspoons Thai fish sauce
juice of 1 lime
3 spring onions, thinly shredded
½ fat red chilli, deseeded and very
   thinly sliced
½ carrot, cut into thin strips
small handful of fresh coriander leaves
2 lime wedges, to serve

Pho, pronounced "Fuh" not "Fo", is probably Vietnam's most famous dish. This light, fragrant soup is perfect for lunch or a light evening meal. Using a pressure cooker enables you to make the time-consuming fragrant broth in a fraction of the time.

Heat the oil in the pressure cooker over a medium heat, add the peppercorns, lemon grass, cinnamon, coriander seeds, star anise and ginger and fry for 1–2 minutes to release their flavours. Add the chicken thighs and measured water.

Lock the lid, bring up to high pressure, stabilize the heat and cook for 10 minutes. Remove from the heat and slow release. Meanwhile, cook the rice noodles according to the packet instructions.

Remove the chicken from the stock. Strain the stock through a sieve into a jug, then return to the cooker. Shred the chicken using 2 forks and return to the stock.

Add the fish sauce, lime juice and spring onions to the cooker and stir.

Divide the noodles between 2 serving bowls. Pour over the soup, then sprinkle over the red chilli, carrot and coriander leaves. Serve immediately with lime wedges to squeeze over.

SERVES: 6
Preparation time: 10 minutes
Cooking time: 11 minutes (High pressure)

MOROCCAN SPICED RED LENTIL SOUP

1 tablespoon olive oil
1 onion, chopped
1 garlic clove, crushed
2 teaspoons grated fresh root ginger
250 g (8 oz) small cauliflower florets
2 carrots, finely chopped
1 red pepper, cored, deseeded and
    chopped
2 teaspoons ras el hanout
1 teaspoon ground cinnamon
½ teaspoon ground turmeric
250 g (8 oz) red lentils, rinsed
½ teaspoon salt
1 litre (1¾ pints) hot vegetable stock
juice of ½ lemon

To serve:
Greek yogurt
harissa paste
chopped fresh coriander

Heat the oil in the pressure cooker over a medium heat, add the onion, garlic and ginger and cook for 3–4 minutes until softened. Stir in the cauliflower, carrots and red pepper, then add the spices and cook for a further 2 minutes.

Add the lentils, salt and hot stock and stir well. Lock the lid, bring up to high pressure, stabilize the heat and cook for 5 minutes. Remove from the heat and slow release.

Check the lentils are tender and simmer for a few more minutes if necessary. Squeeze in the lemon juice, stir well, then serve in bowls with a spoonful of yogurt, drizzled with a little harissa and a handful of coriander.

SERVES: 4
Preparation time: 10 minutes, plus cooling
Cooking time: 10 minutes (High pressure)

THAI FREEKEH SALAD WITH PEANUT AND LIME DRESSING

250 g (9 oz) freekeh
1 tablespoon grated fresh root ginger
1 lemon grass stalk, tough outer layers
    removed and finely chopped
1 teaspoon salt
500 ml (17 fl oz) hot vegetable stock
1 large carrot, cut into thin strips
50 g (2 oz) edamame beans
125 g (4 oz) bean sprouts
50 g (2 oz) mangetout, shredded
¼ cucumber, halved, deseeded and
    thinly sliced

For the dressing:
finely grated zest and juice of 2 limes
3 tablespoons crunchy peanut butter
2 tablespoons dark soy sauce
½–1 teaspoon hot chilli powder

To garnish:
2 tablespoons chopped fresh
    coriander
a few chopped toasted peanuts

Add some shredded cooked chicken or peeled prawns if you fancy.

Place the freekeh in the pressure cooker and toast over a medium heat for 2–3 minutes, then add the ginger, lemon grass, salt and hot stock.

Lock the lid, bring up to high pressure, stabilize the heat and cook for 7 minutes. Remove from the heat and quick release. Half-cover with the lid and leave to cool.

Whisk all the ingredients for the dressing together in a small bowl. Transfer the cooled freekeh to a bowl and stir in the vegetables. Spoon two-thirds of the dressing over the salad and gently toss through.

Divide the salad between 4 plates, then sprinkle with the coriander and a few chopped toasted peanuts. Drizzle with the remaining dressing and serve.

SERVES: 4
Preparation time: 5 minutes
Cooking time: 4 minutes (Low pressure)

SALMON AND CHIVE BAKED EGG POTS

softened butter, for greasing
125 g (4 oz) smoked salmon
150 ml (¼ pint) crème fraîche
2 tablespoons chopped chives
4 eggs
2 tablespoons freshly grated Parmesan cheese
sea salt and freshly cracked black pepper
toast soldiers, to serve

Grease 4 x 150 ml (¼ pint) ramekins and divide the salmon between each to cover the bottom and some of the sides.

Combine the crème fraîche with most of the chives, a little sea salt and some freshly cracked black pepper in a small bowl. Add spoonfuls of the mixture to each ramekin.

Crack an egg into each ramekin, then sprinkle over the Parmesan and remaining chives. Cover the ramekins tightly with foil.

Place the upturned steamer basket in the pressure cooker and add the ramekins (you may need to do this in batches, depending on the width of the ramekins), then pour in enough boiling water to come just below the top of the basket. Lock the lid, bring up to low pressure, stabilize the heat and cook for 4 minutes. Remove from the heat and quick release.

Carefully remove the pots and serve immediately with toast soldiers for dipping.

SERVES: 2
Preparation time: 10 minutes
Cooking time: 10 minutes (Low pressure)

HUEVOS RANCHEROS

softened butter, for greasing
2 small corn tortillas, about 10 cm
    (4 inches) in diameter
2 teaspoons sunflower oil
25 g (1 oz) cooking chorizo, diced
½ small red onion, finely chopped
1 garlic clove, crushed
½ green chilli, deseeded and chopped,
    or to taste
¼ red pepper, cored, deseeded and
    diced
1 ripe tomato, chopped
2 tablespoons chopped fresh
    coriander
2 eggs
1 tablespoon grated Cheddar cheese
salt and freshly ground black pepper

For a speedy cheat use 6 tablespoons fresh salsa sauce, add some chopped coriander and divide between the pots.

Grease 2 x 150 ml (¼ pint) ramekins and line each with a tortilla.

Heat the oil in a small frying pan over a medium heat, add the chorizo, onion, garlic, chilli and red pepper and cook for 2–3 minutes until softened. Stir in the tomato and 1 tablespoon of the coriander and cook for a further 2–3 minutes until the mixture has softened and reduced. Season to taste.

Divide the mixture between the prepared ramekins, then make a well in the centre. Crack an egg into each, then sprinkle over the grated cheese and remaining coriander. Cover the ramekins tightly with foil.

Place the upturned steamer basket in the pressure cooker, add the ramekins, then pour in enough boiling water to come just below the basket. Lock the lid and bring up to low pressure, stabilize the heat and cook for 4 minutes. Remove from the heat and quick release. Carefully remove the ramekins and serve immediately.

SERVES: 6
Preparation time: 5 minutes, plus soaking overnight
Cooking time: about 13 minutes (High pressure)

BAKED BEANS IN TOMATO SAUCE

500 g (1 lb) dried haricot beans, soaked overnight
2 tablespoons olive oil
½ teaspoon salt
2 garlic cloves, crushed
1 small carrot, finely chopped
1 celery stick, finely chopped
400 ml (14 fl oz) tomato passata
2 tablespoons tomato ketchup
salt and freshly ground black pepper
buttered toast, to serve

Drain and rinse the beans and place them in the pressure cooker and pour over enough water to come about 2.5 cm (1 inch) above the beans, then add 1 tablespoon of the oil and the salt. Lock the lid, bring up to high pressure, stabilize the heat and cook for 5 minutes. Remove from the heat and quick release. Drain the beans, reserving 300 ml (½ pint) of the cooking water, and set aside.

Wash the pressure cooker, then heat the remaining oil over a medium heat, add the garlic and fry briefly, stirring, until fragrant. Add the carrot and celery and cook for 2–3 minutes until softened.

Add the passata and ketchup and stir together. Return the beans and the reserved cooking water to the cooker. Season well with salt and pepper and stir. Lock the lid, bring back up to high pressure, stabilize the heat and cook for 5 minutes. Remove from the heat and slow release.

Stir well, so the sauce coats the beans and serve on buttered toast. Any leftover beans can be stored in the refrigerator for up to 3 days.

SERVES: 2–3
Preparation time: 5 minutes
Cooking time: 8 minutes (High pressure)

CROQUE MONSIEUR BAKE

softened butter, for greasing
4 slices of bread
2 tablespoons Dijon mustard
4 thin slices of Gruyère cheese, plus
 25 g (1 oz) grated
2 slices of ham
2 large eggs
125 ml (4 fl oz) milk
salt and freshly ground black pepper

Lightly grease an ovenproof dish large enough to hold the sandwiches, but still fit in the pressure cooker.

Spread one side of each slice of bread with mustard. Make sandwiches by putting each slice of cheese against the mustardy bread, and a slice of ham between them. Cut each sandwich in half to make 2 triangles.

Squish the sandwich triangles into the dish.

Beat the eggs and milk together in a bowl and season with a little salt and pepper. Pour over the sandwiches, then leave to stand for a few minutes before covering with foil.

Place the trivet or upturned steamer basket in the pressure cooker, add the dish, then pour in enough water to come just below the top of the trivet or basket. Lock the lid, bring up to high pressure, stabilize the heat and cook for 5 minutes. Remove from the heat and slow release.

Carefully remove the dish from the cooker and sprinkle with the grated cheese. Preheat the grill to high and grill the sandwiches for 2–3 minutes until lightly browned and bubbling. Serve immediately.

SERVES: 4
Preparation time: 8 minutes
Cooking time: about 11 minutes (High pressure)

POSH SPAGHETTI ON TOAST

1 tablespoon olive oil
1 onion, finely chopped
1 garlic clove, crushed
1 celery stick, finely chopped
400 ml (14 fl oz) tomato passata
2 tablespoons tomato ketchup
1 teaspoon dried oregano
½ teaspoon paprika
200 g (7 oz) dried spaghetti, broken
   into pieces
600 ml (1 pint) hot vegetable stock
salt and freshly ground black pepper

To serve:
4 slices of sourdough toast
freshly grated Parmesan cheese

Heat the oil in the pressure cooker over a medium heat, add the onion and fry briefly, then add the garlic and celery and cook for 2–3 minutes until softened.

Add the passata, ketchup, oregano and paprika, season well and stir together. Add the spaghetti and pour over the hot stock. Do not stir.

Lock the lid, bring up to high pressure, stabilize the heat and cook for 8 minutes. Remove from the heat and quick release. Stir well, half-cover with the lid and leave to stand for 3 minutes.

Serve the spaghetti on toast with some pepper and sprinkled with grated Parmesan.

MIDWEEK MEALS

SERVES: 4
Preparation time: 5 minutes
Cooking time: 20 minutes (High pressure)

CHICKEN TINGA TACOS

1 tablespoon sunflower oil
1 onion, chopped
2 garlic cloves, sliced
8 boneless, skinless chicken thighs
1 teaspoon dried oregano
1 teaspoon ground cumin
1 teaspoon ground cinnamon
2 tablespoons chipotle paste en adobo
150 ml (¼ pint) tomato passata
1 teaspoon red wine vinegar
salt and freshly ground black pepper

To serve:
12 small warmed corn tortillas
choice of toppings, such as guacamole,
**   soured cream, grated cheese, crisp**
**   lettuce, roughly chopped fresh**
**   coriander, lime wedges**

Heat the oil in the pressure cooker over a medium heat, add the onion and garlic and cook for 2–3 minutes until softened.

Increase the heat and add the chicken thighs, season with salt and pepper and brown on all sides. Stir in the oregano, spices and chilli paste and turn until the chicken is coated, then add the passata and vinegar and stir.

Lock the lid, bring up to high pressure, stabilize the heat and cook for 10 minutes. Remove from the heat and slow release.

Using 2 forks, shred the chicken in the cooker. Return to the heat and simmer for about 5 minutes until the sauce has thickened. Place in a bowl.

Serve the chicken on the warmed tortillas and top with your favourite toppings and a squeeze of lime.

SERVES: 6
Preparation time: 5 minutes, plus soaking overnight
Cooking time: 15 minutes (High pressure)

CHILLI CON CARNE

400 g (13 oz) dried kidney beans, soaked overnight
2 tablespoons sunflower oil
½ teaspoon salt
1 bay leaf
500 g (1 lb) minced beef
1 large onion, sliced
2 garlic cloves, crushed
2–3 teaspoons hot chilli powder
1 teaspoon ground cumin
2 teaspoons dried oregano
2 x 400 g (13 oz) cans chopped tomatoes
1 tablespoon tomato ketchup
1 teaspoon cocoa powder
salt and freshly ground black pepper

To serve:
cooked rice
soured cream
chopped fresh coriander

Drain and rinse the beans and place them in the pressure cooker, and pour over enough water to come about 2.5 cm (1 inch) above the beans, then add 1 tablespoon of the oil, the salt and bay leaf. Lock the lid, bring up to high pressure, stabilize the heat and cook for 5 minutes. Remove from the heat and quick release. Drain the beans, reserving 350 ml (12 fl oz) of the cooking water and set aside.

Wash the pressure cooker, then heat the remaining oil over a medium heat, add the mince, onion and garlic and cook for 3–4 minutes until the mince is browned. Add the chilli powder, cumin, oregano, tomatoes, ketchup and cocoa powder. Season, then return the beans and reserved cooking water to the cooker.

Lock the lid, bring back up to high pressure, stabilize the heat and cook for 5 minutes. Remove from the heat and quick release.

Serve with cooked rice, soured cream and a sprinkling of coriander.

SERVES: 4
Preparation time: 5 minutes, plus soaking overnight
Cooking time: 20 minutes (High pressure)

BBQ SAUSAGE AND BEAN STEW

250 g (8 oz) dried cannellini beans,
    soaked overnight
2 tablespoons sunflower oil
½ teaspoon salt
8 sausages
1 celery stick, sliced
1 large leek, trimmed, cleaned and
    sliced
2 large carrots, chopped
400 g (13 oz) can chopped tomatoes
100 ml (3½ fl oz) barbecue sauce
salt and freshly ground black pepper
crusty bread, to serve

Drain and rinse the beans and place them in the pressure cooker and pour over enough water to come about 2.5 cm (1 inch) above the beans, then add 1 tablespoon of the oil and the salt. Lock the lid, bring up to high pressure, stabilize the heat and cook for 5 minutes. Remove from the heat and quick release. Drain the beans, reserving 300 ml (½ pint) of the cooking water, and set aside.

Wash the pressure cooker, then heat the remaining oil over a medium heat and cook the sausages for 2 minutes until lightly browned. Remove from the cooker, then add the celery, leek and carrots and cook for 2–3 minutes until softened.

Add the chopped tomatoes, barbecue sauce, beans, reserved cooking water and sausages. Season well, then lock the lid, bring back up to high pressure, stabilise the heat and cook for 10 minutes. Remove from the heat and slow release.

Serve with crusty bread.

SERVES: 4
Preparation time: 10 minutes
Cooking time: 18 minutes (High pressure)

ONE-POT MEATBALLS WITH SPAGHETTI

2 tablespoons olive oil
250 g (8 oz) dried spaghetti, broken in half
400 ml (14 fl oz) cold water
salt and freshly ground black pepper
basil leaves, to garnish

For the meatballs:
200 g (7 oz) lean minced beef
200 g (7 oz) minced pork
2 tablespoons freshly grated Parmesan cheese, plus extra to serve
2 tablespoons chopped parsley
1 teaspoon dried oregano
1 tablespoon dried breadcrumbs
1 egg, beaten

For the tomato sauce:
1 onion, sliced
1 garlic clove, crushed
400 g (13 oz) can chopped tomatoes
400 ml (14 fl oz) tomato passata
1 teaspoon dried oregano
1 teaspoon caster or granulated sugar

First, make the meatballs. Place the minced beef and pork, Parmesan, parsley, oregano, breadcrumbs and egg in a bowl. Season with a little salt and pepper, then using clean hands or a wooden spoon, squish the mixture together until well combined.

Using your hands, roll the mixture into 20 balls.

Next, make the sauce. Heat 1 tablespoon of the oil in the pressure cooker over a medium heat, add the meatballs, in batches, and cook for 3–4 minutes until lightly browned, then remove from the cooker.

Heat the remaining oil in the cooker over a medium heat, add the onion and garlic and cook for 3–4 minutes until softened. Stir in the chopped tomatoes, passata, oregano and sugar. Season and stir well, then return the meatballs to the cooker and stir well. Add the spaghetti on top, then pour over the measured water to cover the pasta.

Lock the lid, bring up to high pressure, stabilize the heat and cook for 7 minutes. Remove from the heat and quick release. Stir well, then close the lid and leave to stand for 2–3 minutes (the pasta will continue to soften).

Serve in bowls with basil leaves and freshly grated Parmesan.

SERVES: 4
Preparation time: 10 minutes
Cooking time: about 19 minutes (High pressure)

SPELT RISOTTO WITH MUSHROOMS AND GREENS

20 g (¾ oz) dried porcini or wild mushrooms
200 ml (7 fl oz) warm water
1 tablespoon olive oil
15 g (½ oz) butter
1 red onion, sliced
2 garlic cloves, crushed
250 g (8 oz) chestnut mushrooms, sliced
250 g (8 oz) pearled spelt
100 ml (3½ fl oz) white wine
500 ml (17 fl oz) hot vegetable stock
1 teaspoon dried thyme or a few sprigs of thyme
150 g (5 oz) spring greens or kale, tough stems removed and roughly chopped
25 g (1 oz) Parmesan cheese, finely grated, plus extra to serve
salt and freshly ground black pepper

Place the dried mushrooms in a heatproof bowl and pour over the measured water. Set aside.

Heat the oil and butter in the pressure cooker over a medium heat, add the onion and garlic and sweat gently for 4–5 minutes, stirring occasionally, until softened but not coloured.

Stir in the chestnut mushrooms and cook for 3–4 minutes until coloured. Strain the dried mushrooms from the soaking water, reserving the water, and roughly chop.

Stir the spelt into the onion mixture until it is completely coated in the oil, then pour in the wine and simmer for 2–3 minutes until it has completely evaporated.

Add the soaked dried mushrooms, then pour in the hot stock, strained mushroom soaking water and thyme, then season with salt and pepper. Lock the lid, bring up to high pressure, stabilize the heat and cook for 7 minutes. Remove from the heat and quick release.

Meanwhile, put the spring greens or kale in a food processor and blitz until finely chopped, or do this by hand.

Return the pressure cooker to the stove and cook for a few more minutes if the liquid needs reducing. Turn off the heat, then stir in the greens and Parmesan and leave to stand uncovered for a few minutes to wilt the greens.

Serve in bowls with extra cheese and pepper.

SERVES: 4
Preparation time: 10 minutes, plus soaking overnight
Cooking time: 15 minutes (High pressure)

CHIPOTLE SWEET POTATO AND BLACK BEAN CHILLI

250 g (8 oz) black beans, soaked
    overnight
2 tablespoons sunflower oil
½ teaspoon salt
1 large onion, chopped
1 garlic clove, crushed
450 g (14½ oz) sweet potatoes, peeled
    and cut into 2.5 cm (1 inch) chunks
1 large red pepper, cored, deseeded
    and cut into 2.5 cm (1 inch) chunks
1 tablespoon chipotle chilli paste
2 x 400 g (13 oz) cans chopped
    tomatoes
2 tablespoons chopped fresh
    coriander
salt and freshly ground black pepper

To serve:
flour or corn tortillas, or cooked
    long-grain rice
soured cream
guacamole

Drain and rinse the beans and place them in the pressure cooker and pour over enough water to come about 2.5 cm (1 inch) above the beans, then add 1 tablespoon of the oil and the salt. Lock the lid, bring up to high pressure, stabilize the heat and cook for 5 minutes. Remove from the heat and quick release. Drain the beans, reserving 250 ml (8 fl oz) of the cooking water, and set aside.

Wash the pressure cooker, then heat the remaining oil over a medium heat, add the onion and garlic and cook for 2–3 minutes until softened. Stir in the sweet potatoes and red pepper and cook for a further 2 minutes. Stir in the chipotle paste, chopped tomatoes, beans and reserved cooking water.

Lock the lid, bring back up to high pressure, stabilize the heat and cook for 5 minutes. Remove from the heat and slow release. Season to taste.

Stir in the coriander, then serve in bowls with tortillas or rice and a spoonful of soured cream and guacamole.

SERVES: 4
Preparation time: 5 minutes
Cooking time: about 20 minutes (High pressure)

BUTTERNUT SQUASH, SAGE AND PINE NUT RISOTTO

2 tablespoons olive oil

25 g (1 oz) unsalted butter

1 red onion, chopped

1 garlic clove, crushed

350 g (12 oz) peeled butternut squash, cut into 1.5 cm (¾ inch) cubes

25 g (1 oz) pine nuts

8 sage leaves

300 g (10½ oz) risotto rice, such as arborio

100 ml (3 fl oz) white wine

600 ml (1 pint) hot vegetable or chicken stock

25 g (1 oz) Parmesan cheese, freshly grated, plus extra to serve

salt and freshly ground black pepper

To serve:

1 tablespoon olive oil

12 sage leaves

Heat the oil and butter in the pressure cooker over a medium heat, add the onion and garlic and sweat gently for 4–5 minutes until softened but not coloured, stirring occasionally.

Stir in the butternut squash, pine nuts and sage leaves and cook for 1 minute until the pine nuts are starting to colour.

Stir the rice into the onion mixture until it is completely coated in the oil, then stir constantly for a few minutes until the rice is shiny and the edges of the grains start to look transparent.

Pour in the wine and simmer for 2–3 minutes until completely evaporated. Pour in the hot stock and season with salt and pepper. Lock the lid, bring up to high pressure, stabilize the heat and cook for 5 minutes. Remove from the heat and quick release.

Meanwhile, heat 1 tablespoon of oil in a frying pan over a high heat, add the sage leaves and cook for about 30–60 seconds until they sizzle and crisp. Transfer to a plate and set aside.

Stir the grated Parmesan into the risotto and leave to stand uncovered for a few minutes. Serve in bowls with extra Parmesan, the crispy sage leaves and pepper.

SERVES: 4
Preparation time: 5 minutes
Cooking time: 12 minutes (High pressure)

CHICKEN TIKKA MASALA

2 tablespoons sunflower oil
1 large onion, chopped
2 garlic cloves, crushed
2.5 cm (1 inch) piece of fresh root ginger, peeled and grated
500 g (1 lb) chicken breast chunks
2 tablespoons tikka masala curry powder
400 ml (14 fl oz) tomato passata
150 g (5 oz) Greek yogurt or reduced-fat crème fraîche
4 tablespoons chopped fresh coriander
salt and freshly ground black pepper
steamed basmati rice, to serve

Heat the oil in the pressure cooker over a medium heat, add the onion, garlic and ginger and cook for 3–4 minutes, stirring occasionally, until the onion is soft and translucent.

Add the chicken and brown all over, then stir in the curry powder and cook for 1 minute. Stir in the passata. Lock the lid, bring up to high pressure, stabilize the heat and cook for 5 minutes. Remove from the heat and slow release.

Season to taste with salt and pepper, then place over a low heat, and if using yogurt, stir in a tablespoon at a time to prevent curdling, or stir in the crème fraîche.

Stir in the coriander and serve immediately with steamed basmati rice.

SERVES: 4
Preparation time: 10 minutes
Cooking time: about 40 minutes (High pressure)

POT ROAST CHICKEN WITH POTATOES

1.5 kg (3 lb) whole chicken, giblets removed
1 lemon, halved
1 tablespoon sunflower oil
large knob of unsalted butter
4 garlic cloves, peeled but kept whole
500 g (1 lb) baby new potatoes, halved
2 carrots, cut into large chunks
250 ml (8 fl oz) hot chicken stock
125 ml (4 fl oz) dry white wine
a few sprigs of rosemary
2 teaspoons cornflour blended with 4 teaspoons cold water
salt and freshly ground black pepper

Season the chicken with salt and pepper, then add the lemon halves to the cavity. Heat the oil and butter in the pressure cooker over a medium heat, add the chicken and brown on all sides. Remove the chicken from the cooker, transfer to a plate and set aside.

Add the garlic, potatoes and carrots to the cooker, then add the hot stock, wine and rosemary. Place the chicken on top. Lock the lid, bring up to high pressure, stabilize the heat and cook for 30 minutes. Remove from the heat and slow release.

Transfer the chicken to a warmed serving plate and cover with foil. Remove the vegetables with a slotted spoon and add to the serving plate. Discard the rosemary.

Pour any juices from the chicken plate into the cooker, mash up the garlic cloves, then stir in the blended cornflour mixture and simmer for 2–3 minutes until thickened.

Carve the chicken and serve with the vegetables and gravy.

SERVES: 3–4
Preparation time: 15 minutes, plus marinating (optional)
Cooking time: about 9 minutes (High pressure)

VIETNAMESE LEMON GRASS PORK WITH RICE

3 lemon grass stalks, tough outer
   layers removed and chopped
1 shallot, roughly chopped
1 tablespoon Thai fish sauce
juice of 1 lime
1 garlic clove, crushed
2 tablespoons soft brown sugar
2 teaspoons sunflower oil
1 pork tenderloin, about 500 g (1 lb),
   halved widthways
200 g (7 oz) jasmine or basmati rice,
   rinsed
½ teaspoon salt
500 ml (17 fl oz) water
freshly ground black pepper

To serve:
thinly sliced carrot and cucumber
mint leaves
chilli sauce

In a small blender, whizz 2 lemon grass stalks with the shallot, fish sauce, lime juice, garlic, sugar and 1 tablespoon of oil, with a good grinding of black pepper, to make a smooth paste. Place the pork in a shallow non-reactive dish and rub all over with the paste. (You can make this the day before and marinate overnight in the refrigerator.)

Heat the remaining oil in the pressure cooker, add the pork with the marinade and cook on all sides for a few minutes until starting to caramelize. Transfer to the steamer basket.

Place the rice in the pressure cooker, add the salt, measured water and remaining chopped lemon grass. Put the trivet in the cooker and place the pork, in the steamer basket, on top.

Lock the lid, bring up to high pressure, stabilize the heat and cook for 5 minutes. Remove from the heat and slow release.

Fluff the rice in the bottom of the cooker, then thinly slice the pork.

Spoon the rice into bowls, top with the carrot and cucumber and add the slices of pork. Garnish with mint leaves and serve with a little chilli sauce.

SERVES: 4
Preparation time: 5 minutes
Cooking time: about 30 minutes (High pressure)

BALSAMIC-GLAZED PORK STEAKS WITH APPLES

25 g (1 oz) unsalted butter
3 red eating apples, halved and cored
2 small red onions, cut into 8 wedges
1 teaspoon sunflower oil
4 pork loin chops or steaks, about
    1.5 cm (¾ inch) thick
100 ml (3½ fl oz) balsamic vinegar
2 teaspoons honey
2 teaspoons chopped thyme leaves or
    1 teaspoon dried thyme
salt and freshly ground black pepper

To serve:
mashed sweet potatoes
broccoli

Heat the butter in the pressure cooker over a medium heat, add the apple halves and cook for 2–3 minutes until starting to caramelize. Transfer to a large plate. Add the onions to the cooker and cook for a further 2–3 minutes until lightly browned. Transfer to the plate.

Add the oil to the pressure cooker. Season the pork chops or steaks with a little salt and pepper, then add to the cooker and cook for 3–4 minutes on each side until browned. You may need to do this in batches.

Mix the vinegar, honey and thyme together in a shallow dish.

Return the pork, apples and onions to the cooker and pour over the vinegar mixture. Lock the lid, bring up to high pressure, stabilize the heat and cook for 13 minutes. Remove from the heat and slow release.

Divide the pork between plates and serve with mashed sweet potatoes and greens.

SERVES: 4
Preparation time: 15 minutes
Cooking time: 18 minutes (High pressure)

MEATLOAF WITH ONION GRAVY

25 g (1 oz) dried breadcrumbs
100 ml (3½ fl oz) milk
250 g (8 oz) minced beef
250 g (8 oz) minced pork
125 g (4 oz) smoked back bacon rashers,
    finely chopped
1 onion, grated
1 carrot, grated
1 egg, beaten
2 teaspoons Worcestershire sauce
1 tablespoon tomato ketchup
1 teaspoon dried mixed herbs
1 teaspoon English mustard
salt and freshly ground black pepper

For the gravy:
1 large onion, sliced
450 ml (¾ pint) hot beef stock
2 teaspoons cornflour blended with
    4 teaspoons cold water

To serve:
mashed potatoes
peas

Line a 500 g (1 lb) loaf tin, about 18 x 12 cm (7 x 4½ inches) with nonstick baking paper, so it lines the bottom and comes over the sides, making sure it fits the pressure cooker.

Place the breadcrumbs in a bowl and pour over the milk. Set aside.

Place all the remaining ingredients for the meatloaf in a large bowl and squish everything together with clean hands until well combined. Add the soaked breadcrumbs, mix well and season with salt and pepper. Press the mixture into the prepared tin, cover with the overhanging baking paper, then cover the top with foil.

Place the onion and hot stock for the gravy in the pressure cooker, then add the trivet. Place the tin on the trivet. Lock the lid, bring up to high pressure, stabilize the heat and cook for 15 minutes. Remove from the heat and slow release.

Remove the meatloaf and trivet from the cooker. Return the cooker to a medium heat, stir the blended cornflour mixture into the onion mixture and cook for 2–3 minutes until thickened.

Serve the meatloaf in slices with the gravy, mashed potato and peas.

SERVES: 4
Preparation time: 10 minutes
Cooking time: about 12 minutes (High pressure)

LENTIL AND CAULIFLOWER CURRY

1 tablespoon sunflower oil

1 large onion, sliced

1 garlic clove, crushed

1 teaspoon grated fresh root ginger

2 tablespoons tikka or other curry paste

400 g (13 oz) cauliflower florets

2 large carrots, sliced

200 g (7 oz) red lentils, rinsed

450 ml (¾ pint) hot vegetable stock

200 g (7 oz) spinach

4 tablespoons natural yogurt or soya yogurt (coconut flavour is good)

salt and freshly ground black pepper

2 tablespoons chopped fresh coriander, to garnish

naan bread, to serve

Heat the oil in the pressure cooker over a medium heat, add the onion, garlic and ginger and cook for 3–4 minutes until softened. Stir in the curry paste and cook for 1 minute.

Add the cauliflower and carrots and stir in the lentils. Pour over the hot stock. Lock the lid, bring up to high pressure, stabilize the heat and cook for 5 minutes. Remove from the heat and slow release.

Check the lentils are tender and simmer for a few more minutes if necessary. Stir in the spinach to wilt, then stir in the yogurt. Season to taste.

Divide among bowls, garnish with chopped coriander and serve with naan bread.

SERVES: 4
Preparation time: 10 minutes
Cooking time: 9 minutes (High pressure)

CHICKEN PATATAS BRAVAS STYLE

1 tablespoon olive oil
450 g (4½ oz) chicken mini fillets
1 small onion, chopped
1 red chilli, deseeded and finely
   chopped
400 g (13 oz) can chopped tomatoes
125 g (4 oz) drained red peppers from
   a jar, sliced
½ teaspoon caster sugar
½ teaspoon salt
1 teaspoon smoked paprika
1 tablespoon sherry or red wine
   vinegar
100 ml (3½ fl oz) hot chicken stock or
   water
1 kg (2 lb) waxy potatoes, cut into
   1.5 cm (¾ inch) pieces
2 tablespoons chopped flat leaf
   parsley, to garnish
garlic aioli, to serve

Heat the oil in the pressure cooker over a medium heat, add the chicken and onion and cook for about 3 minutes until the onion is golden and soft and the chicken is browned. Add the chilli and cook for a further 1 minute.

Add the tomatoes, peppers, sugar, salt, smoked paprika, vinegar, hot stock or measured water and stir well. Stir in the potatoes.

Lock the lid, bring up to high pressure, stabilize the heat and cook for 5 minutes. Remove from the heat and slow release.

Divide between four plates and serve drizzled with garlic aioli and garnished with parsley.

SERVES: 4
Preparation time: 5 minutes
Cooking time: about 14 minutes (High pressure)

SPICY JAMBALAYA

1 tablespoon sunflower oil
1 onion, chopped
2 celery sticks, chopped
1 garlic clove, crushed
100 g (3½ oz) cooking chorizo, sliced
2 boneless, skinless chicken breasts or
    4 thighs, chopped
1 red pepper, cored, deseeded and
    chopped
1 green pepper, cored, deseeded and
    chopped
1 tablespoon paprika
2 teaspoons dried mixed herbs
225 g (7½ oz) long-grain rice
400 g (13 oz) can chopped tomatoes
450 ml (¾ pint) hot chicken stock
125 g (4 oz) cooked peeled prawns
a few drops of Tabasco sauce
    (optional)
salt and freshly ground black pepper
6 spring onions, chopped, to garnish

Heat the oil in the pressure cooker over a medium heat, add the onion, celery and garlic and cook for 3–4 minutes until softened.

Add the chorizo, chicken and peppers and cook for 2 minutes until the peppers have softened and the chorizo has released its oil.

Add the paprika and herbs, then stir in the rice and cook for a further 1 minute. Stir in the chopped tomatoes and hot stock. Lock the lid, bring up to high pressure, stabilize the heat and cook for 3 minutes. Remove from the heat and slow release.

Stir in the prawns and heat through for 3–4 minutes, then season to taste with salt and pepper and a few drops of Tabasco sauce, if using.

Serve immediately in bowls, garnished with the chopped spring onions.

SERVES: 2
Preparation time: 10 minutes
Cooking time: 5 minutes (High pressure)

SALMON EN PAPILLOTE WITH SESAME AND GINGER

1 tablespoon grated fresh root ginger
1 garlic clove, crushed
2 tablespoons dark soy sauce
2 tablespoons rice wine vinegar
1 teaspoon toasted sesame oil
1 carrot, cut into thin strips
75 g (3 oz) mangetout or sugar snaps,
    halved lengthways
4 spring onions, thinly sliced
2 skinless salmon fillets, about 200 g
    (7 oz) each
2 teaspoons toasted sesame seeds
noodles, to serve

Salmon is steamed in a paper parcel with vegetables and ginger for a tasty speedy supper.

Mix the ginger, garlic, soy sauce, rice wine vinegar and sesame oil together in a small bowl.

Place 2 x 23 cm (9 inch) squares of nonstick baking paper on the work surface and divide the vegetables between them. Place a piece of salmon on top of the vegetables and spoon over the ginger and soy sauce mixture.

Fold over the paper to seal, then place the parcels in the steamer basket. Place the trivet in the pressure cooker, then place the steamer basket on top and pour in enough water to come just below the basket.

Lock the lid, bring up to high pressure, stabilize the heat and cook for 5 minutes. Remove from the heat and quick release.

Transfer the salmon to plates and carefully open up the parcels, then sprinkle over the toasted sesame seeds and serve with noodles.

SERVES: 4
Preparation time: 5 minutes
Cooking time: 8 minutes (High pressure)

COD WITH CHORIZO AND POTATOES

1 tablespoon olive oil

125 g (4 oz) cooking chorizo, diced

400 g (13 oz) new potatoes, cut into bite-sized chunks

75 g (3 oz) red peppers from a jar, drained and sliced

1 tablespoon tomato purée

400 g (13 oz) can cherry tomatoes

100 ml (3½ fl oz) water

4 skinless chunky white fish fillets, such as cod or haddock, about 150 g (5 oz) each

salt and freshly ground black pepper

2 tablespoons chopped parsley, to garnish

broccoli or green beans, to serve

This simple recipe is very easy and fast to cook, so is perfect for a midweek meal.

Heat the oil in the pressure cooker over a medium heat, add the chorizo and cook for 2–3 minutes until it starts to release its oil, then stir in the potatoes and peppers.

Add the tomato purée, tomatoes and measured water, then season with a little salt and pepper.

Arrange the fish fillets over the top. Lock the lid, bring up to high pressure, stabilize the heat and cook for 5 minutes. Remove from the heat and quick release.

Serve the fish on top of the potatoes with a sprinkling of parsley and broccoli or green beans.

SERVES: 4
Preparation time: 5 minutes
Cooking time: about 10 minutes (High pressure)

CREAMY TROUT AND BROCCOLI PASTA

350 g (12 oz) dried penne

600 ml (1 pint) boiling water

200 g (7 oz) Tenderstem broccoli, trimmed into 3.5 cm (1½ inch) lengths

125 g (4 oz) cream cheese

finely grated zest and juice of 1 large lemon

100 g (3½ oz) frozen peas

2 tablespoons chopped dill

250 g (8 oz) hot-smoked rainbow trout fillets, flaked

salt and freshly ground black pepper

rocket salad, to serve

This simple pasta cooks in minutes and is perfect for a quick midweek meal.

Place the pasta in the pressure cooker and pour over the measured water. Season with salt and pepper. Lock the lid, bring up to high pressure, stabilize the heat and cook for 6 minutes. Remove from the heat and quick release.

Meanwhile, cook the broccoli in a saucepan of boiling water for 3 minutes, then drain and set aside.

Place the pressure cooker over a medium heat and stir in the cream cheese and lemon zest and juice, stirring constantly, until the cheese has melted and the sauce has thickened and coated the pasta. Stir in the peas, cooked broccoli, dill and trout and heat through.

Serve immediately with a rocket salad.

SERVES: 2
Preparation time: 15 minutes
Cooking time: 30 minutes (High pressure)

SHREDDED DUCK SALAD WITH MANGO AND POMEGRANATE

2 duck legs
1 teaspoon Chinese five-spice powder
3 tablespoons dark soy sauce
3 tablespoons rice wine vinegar
grated zest and juice of 1 orange
1 teaspoon toasted sesame oil
100 g (3½ oz) watercress
1 mango, stoned, peeled and sliced
¼ cucumber, halved lengthways, deseeded and sliced
4 spring onions, sliced
handful of pomegranate seeds
1 red chilli, deseeded and sliced (optional)

Dry the duck legs with kitchen paper, then rub all over with the five-spice powder. Place in the pressure cooker with the soy sauce, rice wine vinegar and orange zest and juice.

Lock the lid, bring up to high pressure, stabilize the heat and cook for 30 minutes. Remove from the heat and slow release.

Remove the duck legs, then strain the cooking liquid through a sieve. Leave the legs to cool slightly, then shred the meat discarding the skin and bones.

Skim the fat from the reserved cooking liquid, then whisk in the sesame oil.

Arrange the watercress on a large serving plate, add the mango, cucumber and spring onions, then add the duck. Spoon over the cooking liquid, sprinkle over the pomegranate seeds and chilli, if using, and serve immediately.

SERVES: 4
Preparation time: 5 minutes
Cooking time: 10 minutes (High pressure)

EASY MAC 'N' CHEESE WITH BACON AND SPINACH

15 g (½ oz) unsalted butter
6 smoked back bacon rashers, chopped
300 g (10 oz) dried macaroni
600 ml (1 pint) boiling water
200 ml (7 fl oz) evaporated milk
1 teaspoon English mustard
125 g (4 oz) mature Cheddar cheese, grated
125 g (4 oz) baby spinach
salt and freshly ground black pepper
green salad, to serve

Heat the butter in the pressure cooker over a medium heat, add the bacon and cook for 2 minutes until starting to crisp.

Add the macaroni and pour over the measured water. Season with salt and pepper. Lock the lid, bring up to high pressure, stabilize the heat and cook for 6 minutes. Remove from the heat and quick release.

Place the cooker over a medium heat and stir in the evaporated milk, mustard and Cheddar, stirring, until the cheese has melted and the sauce has thickened. Stir in the spinach to wilt.

Serve immediately with a green salad and an extra grind of black pepper on top of the mac 'n' cheese.

GATHERINGS

SERVES: 4
Preparation time: 10 minutes
Cooking time: about 30 minutes (High pressure)

SRI-LANKAN LAMB AND COCONUT CURRY

2 tablespoons sunflower oil
1 onion, sliced
2.5 cm (1 inch) piece of fresh root
    ginger, peeled and chopped
2 garlic cloves, crushed
1 green chilli, chopped, deseeded if
    preferred
1 teaspoon ground turmeric
1 tablespoon madras curry powder
5 green cardamom pods, lightly
    crushed
1 cinnamon stick
8 curry leaves (optional)
750 g (1½ lb) lamb shoulder, cut into
    2.5 cm (1 inch) cubes
400 ml (14 fl oz) can coconut milk
finely grated zest and juice of 2 limes
1 tablespoon cornflour
large handful of fresh coriander,
    chopped
salt and freshly ground black pepper

To serve:
pilau rice
thinly sliced coconut, fresh or flaked

Heat the oil in the pressure cooker over a medium heat, add the onion, ginger, garlic and chilli and cook for 3–4 minutes until softened.

Add the spices and curry leaves (if using) and cook for 1 minute, then stir in the lamb. Cook for a few minutes until the meat is starting to brown, then pour over the coconut milk and the zest and juice of one of the limes. Season with a little salt and pepper.

Lock the lid, bring up to high pressure, stabilize the heat and cook for 20 minutes. Remove from the heat and slow release.

Stir in the remaining lime zest. Blend the cornflour with the remaining lime juice in a small bowl, then stir into the curry. Return the cooker to the heat and simmer for 2–3 minutes until thickened. Stir in half of the coriander.

Serve the curry with rice, the remaining coriander and thinly sliced coconut.

SERVES: 4
Preparation time: 10 minutes, plus chilling
Cooking time: 6 minutes (High pressure)

CRAB POTS

softened butter, for greasing
150 ml (¼ pint) milk
100 ml (3½ fl oz) double cream
100 g (3½ oz) brown crab meat
4 egg yolks
1 teaspoon Dijon mustard
100 g (3½ oz) white crab meat
juice of ½ lemon
small handful of micro herbs or rocket
    leaves
salt and freshly ground black pepper
buttered toast or asparagus spears,
    to serve

Perfect for entertaining, these can be prepared in advance.

Lightly grease 4 x 125 ml (4 fl oz) ramekins. Beat the milk, cream, brown crab meat, egg yolks and Dijon mustard together in a bowl. Season with salt and pepper.

Pass the mixture through a sieve into a measuring jug, pressing all of the liquid out of the crab meat and then pour the mixture into the prepared ramekins. Cover each with a circle of greased nonstick baking paper.

Place the upturned steamer basket in the pressure cooker, pour in enough boiling water to come just below the top of the basket. Lock the lid, bring up to high pressure, stabilize the heat and cook for 6 minutes. Remove from the heat and quick release. Remove from the pots and leave to cool slightly, then chill in the refrigerator until ready to serve.

When ready to serve, toss the white crab meat with the lemon juice in a bowl. Spoon over the crab custards, sprinkle with the micro herbs or rocket and serve with buttered toast or asparagus.

SERVES: 4 as a main or 6 as a starter
Preparation time: 5 minutes
Cooking time: 25 minutes (High pressure)

CHORIZO AND SQUID STEW

2 tablespoons olive oil
500 g (1 lb) prepared squid rings
1 onion, chopped
½ teaspoon smoked paprika
125 g (4 oz) cooking chorizo, sliced
2 garlic cloves, sliced
150 ml (¼ pint) white wine
a few sprigs of thyme
strip of lemon rind
400 g (13 oz) can chopped tomatoes
salt and freshly ground black pepper
chopped flat leaf parsley, to garnish
crusty or garlic bread, to serve

This makes a perfect main or could be a starter or appetizer.

Heat the oil in the pressure cooker over a high heat, add the squid and cook for 3–4 minutes until lightly browned. Transfer to a plate and set aside.

Add the onion, paprika and chorizo to the cooker, reduce the heat to medium and cook until the chorizo has released its oil.

Return the squid to the cooker, then add all the remaining ingredients. Season with a little salt and pepper.

Lock the lid, bring up to high pressure, stabilize the heat and cook for 20 minutes. Remove from the heat and slow release.

Divide among shallow bowls, garnish with parsley and serve with crusty or garlic bread to mop up the juices.

SERVES: 6
Preparation time: 10 minutes
Cooking time: about 1 hour (High pressure)

KOREAN BEEF SHORT RIBS

6 beef short ribs, trimmed of excess
 fat
1 tablespoon toasted sesame oil
2 onions, chopped
2 garlic cloves, crushed
150 ml (¼ pint) hot beef stock
100 ml (3½ fl oz) dark soy sauce
100 ml (3½ fl oz) barbecue sauce
2 tablespoons honey
2 tablespoons gochujang (Korean chilli
 paste)
2 small pears, peeled, cored and
 whizzed
1 tablespoon cornflour blended with
 2 tablespoons cold water
freshly ground black pepper

To serve:
steamed rice
shredded spring onions
kimchi

This recipe is only suitable for a 6 litre (10½ pint) pressure cooker, but if you only have a smaller cooker, then you can also make it using 3–4 ribs and ½ of the ingredients instead.

Season the beef with pepper. Heat the oil in the pressure cooker over a medium heat, add the ribs and cook, in batches, for about 3–4 minutes until lightly browned on all sides. Transfer to a plate.

Add the onions and garlic to the cooker and cook for 1 minute until starting to soften, then stir in all the remaining ingredients, except the blended cornflour. Return the ribs to the cooker.

Lock the lid, bring up to high pressure, stabilize the heat and cook for 50 minutes. Remove from the heat and slow release.

Transfer the ribs to a warmed plate. Add the blended cornflour to the sauce and stir over a high heat until it starts to boil, then reduce to medium and simmer for 5 minutes.

Place the ribs on the cooked rice with the sauce poured over the top. Garnish with spring onions and serve with a side of kimchi.

SERVES: 6–8
Preparation time: 15 minutes, plus marinating (optional)
Cooking time: about 1 hour 45 minutes (High pressure)

LAMB SHAWARMA

3 tablespoons groundnut or sunflower
    oil
1.5 kg (3 lb 5 oz) boned and rolled
    shoulder of lamb
200 ml (7 fl oz) water

For the spice paste:
3 garlic cloves, crushed
25 g (1 oz) piece of fresh root ginger,
    peeled and grated
1 tablespoon ground coriander
1 tablespoon ground cumin
1 teaspoon ground cardamom
1 teaspoon ground cinnamon
1 teaspoon cayenne pepper
1 tablespoon smoked paprika
¼ teaspoon ground cloves
1 teaspoon salt
1 teaspoon ground black pepper
4 tablespoons lemon juice

To serve:
flatbreads
shredded lettuce
tomato and cucumber salad

This is perfect for entertaining a group of friends. Serve with flatbreads and a fresh tomato and cucumber salad. It looks like a long list of spices, but it's well worth it. This recipe would take 4–5 hours in the oven.

Mix all the ingredients for the spice paste with 2 tablespoons of the oil in a bowl. Rub this all over and into the rolled lamb. If liked, cover and leave to marinate in the refrigerator for a few hours or overnight.

Heat the remaining oil in the pressure cooker over a medium heat, add the meat and sear on all sides. Pour in the measured water, then lock the lid, bring up to high pressure, stabilize the heat and cook for 1½ hours. Remove from the heat and slow release.

Remove the lamb and cover with foil. Leave to rest for 10 minutes. Before covering with foil, if liked, place on the barbecue or in a hot oven pre-heated 200°C (400°F), Gas Mark 6, for 5 minutes to crisp up the skin.

Meanwhile, return the pressure cooker to the heat and reduce down the juices.

Using 2 forks, shred the lamb, then serve on flatbreads, drizzled with the reduced pan juices and shredded lettuce and salad.

SERVES: 6
Preparation time: 20 minutes
Cooking time: about 1 hour 45 minutes (High pressure)

PULLED PORK

1.5 kg (3 lb) boneless pork shoulder joint, rind removed
1 tablespoon salt
2 tablespoons dark muscovado sugar
1 tablespoon smoked paprika
1 tablespoon sunflower oil
200 ml (7 fl oz) apple juice
1 tablespoon cornflour blended with 2 tablespoons cold water

To serve:
brioche rolls
coleslaw

Pulled pork can take up to 6 hours in the oven. You can also crisp up the cooked pork on the barbecue, if liked.

Pat the pork dry with kitchen paper. Mix the salt, sugar and paprika together in a small bowl. Unroll the pork and rub half the mix thoroughly all over the pork, reserving the other half. Roll up the pork and secure with kitchen string.

Heat the oil in a large frying pan over a medium heat, add the pork and gently brown on all sides. Transfer the pork to the pressure cooker. If the pork is too long cut it in half widthways. Pour in the apple juice, then lock the lid, bring up to high pressure, stabilize the heat and cook for 1½ hours. Remove from the heat and slow release.

Remove the pork. Add the blended cornflour to the sauce in the cooker along with the reserved seasoning mix. Bring to the boil, then reduce the heat and simmer for 5 minutes until thickened and reduced.

Remove the string from the pork and shred with 2 forks into chunky pieces. Return the pulled pork to the sauce in the cooker and stir well. Serve the pulled pork in the brioche rolls with coleslaw.

SERVES: 6
Preparation time: 10 minutes
Cooking time: about 25 minutes (High pressure)

CHICKEN WITH PRESERVED LEMON AND OLIVES

2 tablespoons olive oil

2 onions, sliced

2 garlic cloves, crushed

1 teaspoon ground cumin

1 teaspoon ground ginger

½ teaspoon ground paprika

½ teaspoon ground cinnamon

6 skinless chicken legs

600 ml (1 pint) hot chicken stock

generous pinch of saffron threads
    soaked in 1 tablespoon water

juice of ½ lemon

2 preserved lemons, each halved, pith
    removed, then skin cut into thin
    strips, plus extra strips to serve

20 green olives, pitted

25 g (1 oz) fresh coriander, chopped

25 g (1 oz) flatleaf parsley, chopped

15 g (½ oz) butter

salt and freshly ground black pepper

couscous, to serve

Heat the oil in the pressure cooker over a medium heat, add the onions and garlic and cook for 2–3 minutes until softened.

Stir in the spices and cook for 1 minute, then add the chicken. Pour over the hot stock, saffron water and lemon juice, then add the preserved lemon strips, olives and herbs and season well.

Lock the lid, bring up to high pressure, stabilize the heat and cook for 15 minutes. Remove from the heat and quick release.

Transfer the chicken to warmed plates. Add the butter to the sauce in the cooker and simmer over a low heat for 4–5 minutes until slightly reduced.

Serve the chicken on the couscous, with the sauce poured over and sprinkled with extra preserved lemon.

SERVES: 6
Preparation time: 15 minutes
Cooking time: about 40 minutes (High pressure)

BEEF RENDANG

1 tablespoon sunflower oil
1 cinnamon stick
1 star anise
2 lemon grass stalks, tough outer layers removed and chopped
4 kaffir lime leaves, roughly torn
1.5 kg (3 lb) braising steak, cut into 2.5 cm (1 inch) chunks
400 g (134 oz) can coconut milk
2 teaspoons palm or soft brown sugar
salt and freshly ground black pepper

For the spice paste:
2 onions, roughly chopped
6 garlic cloves, crushed
2.5 cm (1 inch) piece of fresh root ginger, peeled and chopped
6 dried Kashmiri chillies, stalks removed
2 tablespoons tamarind paste
1 teaspoon ground turmeric
2 teaspoons ground coriander
1 teaspoon ground cumin

To serve:
steamed rice
crispy shallots
fresh coriander leaves

Place all the ingredients for the spice paste in a food processor and blitz until it forms a rough paste.

Heat the oil in the pressure cooker over a medium heat, add the paste, cinnamon stick, star anise, lemon grass and kaffir lime leaves, season with salt and pepper and cook, stirring, for 5 minutes.

Add the beef and cook for 5 minutes, or until beginning to brown, stirring to make sure the meat is coated in the paste.

Stir in the coconut milk. Lock the lid, bring up to high pressure, stabilize the heat and cook for 25 minutes. Remove from the heat and slow release.

Return the cooker to the heat and reduce the sauce to your desired consistency. Stir in the sugar, remove the cinnamon stick and star anise and serve the rendang with rice, crispy shallots and coriander leaves.

SERVES: 6
Preparation time: 10 minutes, plus marinating
Cooking time: 40 minutes (High pressure)

DUCK WITH PLUM SAUCE AND STAR ANISE

6 duck legs
4 tablespoons dark soy sauce
2 teaspoons Chinese five-spice powder
3 whole star anise
1 tablespoon grated fresh root ginger
1 teaspoon Szechuan pepper, crushed
1 cinnamon stick
1 tablespoon olive oil
500 g (1 lb) plums, stoned and halved
75 ml (2 fl oz) white wine vinegar
1–2 red chillies, deseeded and sliced
50 g (1 oz) soft brown sugar
1 tablespoon cornflour blended with
   2 tablespoons cold water

To serve:
rice
Chinese greens

Place the duck legs in a large food bag with the soy sauce, five-spice powder, star anise, ginger, Szechuan pepper, cinnamon and oil, then seal and leave to marinate in the refrigerator for at least 2 hours, or overnight.

When ready to cook, place the plums, vinegar, chillies and sugar in the pressure cooker, then pour the marinade from the bag over the top. Stir together and place the duck legs on top.

Lock the lid, bring up to high pressure, stabilize the heat and cook for 35 minutes. Remove from the heat and slow release.

Transfer the duck to warmed plates. Discard the star anise and cinnamon stick, then stir the blended cornflour into the sauce in the cooker. Bring to the boil, then reduce the heat and simmer for 2–3 minutes until thickened.

Serve with cooked rice and greens, with the plum sauce poured over the top.

SERVES: 2
Preparation time: 15 minutes
Cooking time: 6 minutes (High pressure)

SEA BREAM WITH COCONUT AND THAI HERBS

2 small sea bream or sea bass, about
   300 g (10 oz) each, cleaned and
   scaled, banana leaves or nonstick
   baking paper
sunflower oil, for brushing
100 g (3 oz) basmati rice
½ teaspoon salt
250 ml (8 fl oz) water

For the paste:
1–2 Thai green chillies, deseeded and
   chopped
1 lemon grass stalk, tough outer layers
   removed and chopped
2.5 cm (1 inch) piece of fresh root
   ginger, peeled and chopped
2 garlic cloves, crushed
25 g (1 oz) fresh coriander
25 g (1 oz) Thai basil or mint
3 kaffir lime leaves
½ teaspoon Thai fish sauce
1 teaspoon ground cumin
juice of 1 lime, plus wedges to serve
100 ml (3½ fl oz) coconut cream
salt and freshly ground black pepper

Whole fish is flavoured with Thai herbs and spices and then encased in banana leaves. Don't worry if you can't get hold of banana leaves, just wrap the fish in nonstick baking paper.

To make the paste, place all the ingredients, except the cumin, lime juice and coconut cream, in a food processor and blend to a paste. Add the cumin, lime juice and coconut cream and season with salt and pepper.

Make sure the fish fit in the pressure cooker. If necessary, remove the heads or tails. Make a few diagonal slits through the skin on both sides of each fish, then rub over the paste. Lightly brush the banana leaves or nonstick baking paper with oil. Place each fish in the middle and wrap in the leaves or paper to enclose the fish completely, securing with cocktail sticks if using banana leaves.

Place the rice the pressure cooker and add the salt and measured water. Put the trivet or upturned steamer basket in the cooker and place the fish parcels on top.

Lock the lid, bring up to high pressure, stabilize the heat and cook for 6 minutes. Remove from the heat and slow release.

Carefully remove the parcels, then unwrap the fish and serve with the rice and a lime wedge.

SERVES: 6
Preparation time: 15 minutes
Cooking time: 1 hour 15 minutes (High pressure)

BEEF CHEEKS WITH PORCINI MUSHROOMS AND RED WINE

50 g (2 oz) dried porcini mushrooms
250 ml (8 fl oz) warm water
2 tablespoons plain flour
1.5 kg (3 lb) beef cheeks, halved if large
3 tablespoons olive oil
2 red onions, sliced
2 garlic cloves, crushed
2 celery sticks, sliced
300 ml (½ pint) full-bodied red wine
250 g (8 oz) chestnut mushrooms
400 g (13 oz) can chopped tomatoes
a few sprigs of thyme
1 tablespoon cornflour blended with
    2 tablespoons cold water
salt and freshly ground black pepper

To serve:
buttery mash
carrots and greens

This rich beef stew is perfect for entertaining. Beef cheeks take up to 4 hours to become tender in the oven, but will be meltingly tender in 1 hour in the pressure cooker.

Place the dried mushrooms in a heatproof bowl and pour over the warm measured water. Set aside.

Meanwhile, season the flour with a little salt and pepper, spread out on a plate and use to coat the beef cheeks. Heat 2 tablespoons of the oil in the pressure cooker over a medium heat, add the meat and cook, in batches, until browned, then transfer to a plate.

Add the remaining oil to the cooker, then add the onions, garlic and celery and cook over a low heat for 3–4 minutes until softened. Return the beef to the cooker and pour over the wine.

Strain the porcini mushrooms over a jug to remove any grit, reserving the soaking water, then add both to the cooker with the chestnut mushrooms, tomatoes and thyme. Season well.

Lock the lid, bring up to high pressure, stabilize the heat and cook for 1 hour. Remove from the heat and slow release. Thicken the sauce over a low heat with the cornflour, if necessary.

Serve the beef with buttery mash, carrots and greens.

SERVES: 6–8
Preparation time: 10 minutes
Cooking time: 25 minutes (High pressure)

BOURBON-GLAZED BUFFALO WINGS WITH BLUE CHEESE DIP

1.5 kg (3 lb) chicken wings

For the sauce:
100 ml (3½ fl oz) tomato ketchup
75 ml (3 fl oz) cider vinegar
100 ml (3½ fl oz) bourbon
4 tablespoons light brown sugar
1 tablespoon hot chilli sauce
1 tablespoon Worcestershire sauce
2 teaspoons smoked paprika
salt and freshly ground black pepper

For the blue cheese dip:
125 g (4½ oz) blue cheese, such as Gorgonzola or Dolcelatte
150 ml (¼ pint) soured cream
2 teaspoons lemon juice
1 tablespoon chopped chives

Place all the ingredients for the sauce in the pressure cooker and bring to the boil, then reduce the heat and simmer for 2 minutes. Add the chicken wings and stir until they are coated in the sauce. Lock the lid, bring up to high pressure, stabilize the heat and cook for 10 minutes. Remove from the heat and quick release.

Meanwhile, mash all the ingredients for the dip together in a bowl with a fork until well combined. Set aside.

Preheat the grill to high and line a baking tray with foil. Transfer the wings to the tray. Place the pressure cooker over a high heat and boil the sauce for 5 minutes, or until reduced. Pour the sauce over the wings, turning to coat.

Place the baking tray under the grill and cook for 5 minutes, turning occasionally and basting with the sauce, until sticky.

Transfer the wings to a shallow bowl or plate, pour over any leftover sauce and serve with the blue cheese dip.

SERVES: 4
Preparation time: 10 minutes
Cooking time: 22 minutes (High pressure)

TOULOUSE SAUSAGES WITH PUY LENTILS

1 tablespoon olive oil
8 Toulouse sausages
125 g (4 oz) smoked pancetta, cubed
1 onion, sliced
1 celery stick, diced
1 carrot, diced
125 ml (4 fl oz) red wine
250 g (8 oz) can Puy lentils, rinsed
150 ml (¼ pint) hot chicken stock
2 teaspoons thyme leaves, chopped
1 bay leaf
freshly ground black pepper
cavolo nero, cabbage or kale, to serve

Perfect for entertaining, there is no need to add extra salt as the bacon is quite salty.

Heat the oil in the pressure cooker over a medium heat, add the sausages and lightly brown on all sides, then transfer to a plate.

Add the pancetta and cook until crispy, then stir in the onion, celery and carrot. Cook for 2–3 minutes until softened.

Pour in the wine, stirring to deglaze the cooker (scraping and stirring the browned bits from the bottom over a medium-high heat to melt all the cooking residues into the wine). Simmer for 3–4 minutes to reduce by half. Stir in the lentils and hot stock, then return the sausages to the cooker. Add the thyme and bay leaf and season with pepper.

Lock the lid, bring up to high pressure, stabilize the heat and cook for 8 minutes. Remove from the heat and slow release.

Check the lentils are tender and simmer for a few minutes, if necessary. Serve with cavolo nero, cabbage or kale.

SIDES AND PRESERVES

SERVES: 4
Preparation time: 10 minutes
Cooking time: 8 minutes (High pressure)

BOMBAY POTATOES

2 tablespoons sunflower oil
1 large onion, sliced
1 tablespoon grated fresh root ginger
2 garlic cloves, crushed
1 teaspoon cumin seeds
1 teaspoon black mustard seeds
½ teaspoon ground turmeric
2 teaspoons ground coriander
1 teaspoon garam masala
1 teaspoon hot chilli powder
550 g (1¼ lb) potatoes, peeled and cut
    into 2 cm (¾ inch) pieces
2 tomatoes, roughly chopped
4 tablespoons water
salt and freshly ground black pepper
large handful of coriander leaves,
    chopped, to garnish

Heat the oil in the pressure cooker over a medium heat, add the onion, ginger and garlic and cook for 2–3 minutes until softened. Add all the spices and stir for 2 minutes until the mustard seeds start to pop.

Stir in the potatoes and turn to coat in the spice oil. Add the tomatoes and measured water and season with salt and pepper.

Lock the lid, bring up to high pressure, stabilize the heat and cook for 3 minutes. Remove from the heat and quick release.

Serve garnished with coriander.

SERVES: 4
Preparation time: 2 minutes
Cooking time: 5 minutes (High pressure)

LEMON PILAU RICE

1 tablespoon sunflower oil
1 teaspoon black mustard seeds
4 green cardamom pods, lightly
    crushed
8 fresh or dried curry leaves
200 g (7 oz) basmati rice
finely grated zest and juice of 2 lemons
pinch of saffron threads soaked in
    1 tablespoon warm water
500 ml (17 fl oz) water
½ teaspoon salt

This rice makes a perfect accompaniment to curries.

Heat the oil in the pressure cooker over a medium heat, add the spices and curry leaves and fry for 1–2 minutes until the mustard seeds start to pop.

Add the rice, lemon zest, saffron in its soaking water, measured water and salt. Lock the lid, bring up to high pressure, stabilize the heat and cook for 3 minutes. Remove from the heat and slow release.

Stir in the lemon juice, separate the grains with a fork and serve as an accompaniment to curries and stews.

SERVES: 6
Preparation time: 10 minutes
Cooking time: 10 minutes (High pressure)

POTATO BOULANGÈRE

2 tablespoons olive oil

2 onions, thinly sliced

a few sprigs of thyme or rosemary

1.25 kg (2½ lb) floury potatoes, such as
Maris Piper or Desirée, peeled and
sliced about 2.5 mm (⅛ inch) thick

400 ml (14 fl oz) hot chicken or
vegetable stock

25 g (1 oz) butter, plus extra for
greasing

salt and freshly ground black pepper

This is delicious as an accompaniment to roast meats.

Heat the oil in the pressure cooker over a medium heat, add the onions and herbs and cook for about 5 minutes until softened and lightly coloured. Transfer to a plate and set aside.

Spread a layer of potatoes over the bottom of the cooker. Sprinkle over a few onions and continue layering, seasoning with a little salt and pepper and finishing with a layer of potatoes.

Pour over the hot stock. Lock the lid, bring up to high pressure, stabilize the heat and cook for 3 minutes. Remove from the heat and quick release.

Meanwhile, preheat the grill to high. Grease a shallow 2 litre (3½ pint) roasting tin. Carefully transfer the potato mixture into the tin, dot with a little butter, then cook under the hot grill until the top is slightly golden.

SERVES: 4–6
Preparation time: 5 minutes, plus soaking overnight
Cooking time: about 10 minutes (High pressure)

WHITE BEAN AND GARLIC MASH

300 g (10½ oz) dried cannellini beans,
  soaked overnight
3 tablespoons olive oil, plus a little
  extra for drizzling
1 teaspoon salt
6 garlic cloves, peeled but kept whole
2 tablespoons chopped rosemary
finely grated zest and juice of 1 large
  lemon
salt and freshly ground black pepper

This is delicious made with smoked garlic if you can get it.

Drain and rinse the beans and place them in the pressure cooker and pour over enough water to come about 2.5 cm (1 inch) above the beans. Then add 1 tablespoon of the oil and the salt. Lock the lid, bring up to high pressure, stabilize the heat and cook for 15 minutes. Remove from the heat and quick release. Drain the beans, reserving 400 ml (14 fl oz) of the cooking water, and set aside.

Wash the pressure cooker, then heat the remaining oil over a medium heat, add the garlic and rosemary and fry briefly, stirring, until fragrant.

Return the beans and reserved cooking water to the cooker and stir well. Lock the lid, bring back up to high pressure, stabilize the heat and cook for 10 minutes. Remove from the heat and slow release.

Mash the beans with a potato masher, then stir in the lemon zest and juice. Season to taste. Serve drizzled with a little extra oil, if liked.

SERVES: 4
Preparation time: 5 minutes
Cooking time: 12 minutes (High pressure)

MUNG DHAL WITH CURRY LEAVES AND TAMARIND

1 tablespoon sunflower or groundnut
  oil
2 onions, chopped
2 garlic cloves, crushed
2.5 cm (1 inch) piece of fresh root
  ginger, peeled and grated
1–2 green chillies, halved lengthways
  and deseeded
10–12 curry leaves
1 teaspoon black mustard seeds
1 cinnamon stick
1 teaspoon ground cumin
1 teaspoon ground coriander
½ teaspoon ground turmeric
200 g (7 oz) tomatoes,chopped
1 teaspoon tamarind paste
250g (8 oz) yellow mung dhal
600 ml (1 pint) hot vegetable stock
salt and freshly ground black pepper

To serve:
a few fried curry leaves
lime wedges

The tamarind gives this dhal a slightly sour taste. Serve with naan bread or as an accompaniment to curries.

Heat the oil in the pressure cooker over a medium heat, add the onions, garlic and ginger and cook for 3–4 minutes until softened.

Add the chillies, curry leaves and spices and cook for 2–3 minutes until the mustard seeds start to pop. Stir in the chopped tomatoes, tamarind paste, mung dhal and hot stock. Season with salt and pepper.

Lock the lid, bring up to high pressure, stabilize the heat and cook for 5 minutes. Remove from the heat and slow release.

Stir well and season to taste. Serve immediately with a few fried curry leaves and lime wedges to squeeze over.

SERVES: 6—8
Preparation time: 10 minutes, plus cooling
Cooking time: 4 minutes (High pressure)

HERBED TABBOULEH WITH POMEGRANATE SEEDS

150 g (5 oz) bulgur wheat
1 tablespoon olive oil
450 ml (¾ pint) hot vegetable stock
1 teaspoon salt
1 tablespoon pomegranate molasses
finely grated zest and juice of 1 lemon
1 teaspoon harissa paste
¼ cucumber, deseeded and diced
125 g (4 oz) radishes, finely sliced
350 g (12 oz) tomatoes, deseeded and
   diced
200 g (7 oz) pomegranate seeds
4 tablespoons chopped mint
4 tablespoons chopped flat leaf
   parsley
salt and freshly ground black pepper

This tabbouleh makes a perfect accompaniment to any of the pulled meats in this book.

Place the bulgur wheat in the pressure cooker, add the oil, hot stock and salt. Lock the lid, bring up to high pressure, stabilize the heat and cook for 4 minutes. Remove from the heat and slow release. Transfer the bulgur wheat mixture to a large bowl.

Meanwhile, mix the pomegranate molasses, lemon zest and juice and harissa paste together in a small bowl. Pour over the wheat, mix well and leave to cool.

When the wheat has cooled, fluff with a fork to separate the grains, then stir in all the remaining ingredients. Season to taste and serve.

SERVES: 4
Preparation time: 10 minutes
Cooking time: 7 minutes (High pressure)

CREAMY CELERIAC MASH

1 large celeriac, peeled and cut into
   2.5 cm (1 inch) chunks, about 1 kg
   (2 lb) peeled weight
3 garlic cloves, peeled but kept whole
300 ml (½ pint) hot vegetable stock
½ teaspoon salt
2 tablespoons double cream
knob of butter
pinch of grated nutmeg
salt and freshly ground black pepper

This celeriac mash makes a great alternative to traditional mashed potato. It's delicious served with stews.

Place the celeriac, garlic, hot stock and salt in the pressure cooker.

Lock the lid, bring up to high pressure, stabilize the heat and cook for 7 minutes. Remove from the heat and slow release.

Drain off the liquid and return the celeriac and garlic to the cooker, mash with a potato masher until smooth, then stir in the cream, butter and a little nutmeg. Season to taste.

SERVES: 4
Preparation time: 2 minutes
Cooking time: 20–22 minutes (High pressure)

BAKED SWEET POTATOES

4 sweet potatoes
1 tablespoon olive oil
1 teaspoon sea salt

Pressure cooking the sweet potatoes makes them extremely soft and fluffy. Baking them helps crisp the skin and brings out the sweetness. These are perfect as a side or fill with your favourite fillings.

Prick the sweet potatoes all over with a fork. Place the steamer basket in the pressure cooker, add the potatoes, (it doesn't matter if they sit on top of each other), then pour in enough water to come just below the basket.

Lock the lid, bring up to high pressure, stabilize the heat and cook for 15 minutes. Remove from the heat and quick release.

Meanwhile, preheat the oven to 200°C (400°F), Gas Mark 6. Mix the oil and salt together on a baking tray and place the tray in the oven to preheat. Remove the potatoes with tongs and roll in the oil and salt mixture.

Bake for 5–7 minutes until the skin is crisp. Serve immediately.

SERVES: 8–10 slices
Preparation time: 10 minutes
Cooking time: 15 minutes (High pressure)

CORNBREAD

300 ml (½ pint) buttermilk
50 g (2 oz) butter, melted and cooled ,
    plus extra for greasing
250 g (98oz) coarse cornmeal (polenta)
1 tablespoon baking powder
1 teaspoon salt
125 g (4 oz) canned sweetcorn kernels,
    from a can, drained
5 spring onions, finely chopped
2 large eggs

To add a spicy kick to this dish, you could serve it with a sprinkling of chopped red chilli, if you like. Serve with the Chilli Con Carne (see page 36).

Grease a 15 cm (6 inch) cake tin (about 7 cm (3 inches) deep) and line the base with nonstick baking paper.

In a large mixing bowl, place the cornmeal (polenta), baking powder, salt, sweetcorn kernels and spring onions. Mix well with a wooden spoon.

In a measuring jug, whisk together the eggs, buttermilk and melted butter.

Pour the egg mixture into the dry ingredients and stir well to combine.

Pour the mixture into the prepared tin. Place the trivet or upturned steamer basket in the pressure cooker, add the tin then pour in enough water to come just below the top of the trivet or basket. Lock the lid, bring up to high pressure, stabilize the heat and cook for 15 minutes. Remove from the heat and slow release.

Remove the cornbread from the cooker and leave to cool in the tin for 10 minutes. The bread is delicious served while still warm or cold in thick slices. Any remaining cornbread can be stored in an airtight container for up to 2 days.

MAKES: 4 x 250 g (8 oz) jars
Preparation time: 10 minutes
Cooking time: about 30 minutes (High pressure)

TOMATO AND CHILLI JAM

750 g (1½ lb) tomatoes, halved
2.5 cm (1 inch) piece of fresh root
   ginger, peeled and chopped
2 garlic cloves, chopped
2 large mild red chillies, roughly
   chopped, deseeded if preferred
275 g (9 oz) soft light brown sugar
6 tablespoons red wine vinegar
½ teaspoon salt

This jam is delicious served with cheese or cold meats. To sterilize jars, wash in hot soapy water, rinse, then dry in an oven preheated to 150°C (300°F), Gas Mark 2. Alternatively, run through a dishwasher on its hottest setting.

Place the tomatoes, ginger, garlic and chillies in a food processor and blend until fairly smooth. Pour into the pressure cooker and add the sugar, vinegar and salt.

Stir over a medium heat until the sugar has dissolved, then lock the lid, bring up to high pressure, stabilize the heat and cook for 7 minutes. Remove from the heat and slow release.

Place the cooker over a high heat, bring the mixture to the boil, then reduce the heat and simmer for 15–20 minutes until thickened and glossy, stirring occasionally.

Pour into sterilized jars (see introduction) and seal with the lids. It will keep for up to 3 months in the refrigerator, and for up to 1 month after opening.

MAKES: 4 x 250 g (8 oz) jars
Preparation time: 10 minutes
Cooking time: about 25 minutes (High pressure)

MANGO CHUTNEY

1 tablespoon sunflower oil
1 small onion, finely chopped
2.5 cm (1 inch) piece of fresh root
    ginger, peeled and finely chopped
1 teaspoon cumin seeds
1 teaspoon ground turmeric
½ teaspoon nigella seeds
4 cardamom pods, seeds crushed
2 unripe mangoes, stoned, peeled and
    cut into 2.5 cm (1 inch) pieces
1 small cooking apple, about 200 g
    (7 oz), peeled, cored and cut into
    small pieces
250 ml (8 fl oz) cider vinegar
175 g (6 oz) soft light brown sugar

This mango chutney will keep unopened for up to 6 months in the cool, dark place.

Heat the oil in the pressure cooker over a medium heat, add the onion and ginger and cook for 2–3 minutes until softened. Add the spices and cook for a further 1 minute.

Add the mangoes, apple, vinegar and sugar and stir until the sugar starts to dissolve. Lock the lid, bring up to high pressure, stabilize the heat and cook for 5 minutes. Remove from the heat and slow release.

Place the pressure cooker over a medium heat and simmer the mixture for 12–15 minutes until reduced and thickened.

Ladle into warmed sterilized jars (see page 98), cover each with a waxed paper disc and seal with the lids. Store in a cool, dark place. Refrigerate for up to 1 month after opening.

MAKES: 2 x 250 g (8 oz) jars
Preparation time: 10 minutes
Cooking time: 10 minutes (High pressure)

PASSION FRUIT CURD

6–8 ripe passion fruits, halved and
    pulp removed
3 eggs
2 egg yolks
200 g (7 oz) caster sugar
1 tablespoon lemon juice
150 g (5 oz) unsalted butter, cubed

This curd will keep for up to 1 month in the refrigerator. Once opened, use within a week. It's delicious spread on toast or as a filling for cakes or meringues.

Put the passion fruit pulp in a food processor and whizz to separate the seeds from all the juicy bits. Scrape into a sieve set over a jug, pushing through as much pulp as you can. You should have 200 ml (7 fl oz). Reserve 2 tablespoons of the seeds, then discard the rest.

Beat the eggs together in a heatproof bowl, then add the sugar and mix thoroughly. Stir in the remaining ingredients.

Loosely cover the bowl with nonstick baking paper. Place the trivet in the pressure cooker and pour in enough water so it doesn't touch the base of the bowl. Place the bowl on the trivet.

Lock the lid, bring up to high pressure, stabilize the heat and cook for 10 minutes. Remove from the heat and slow release.

Carefully remove the bowl, then whisk vigorously to fully incorporate the butter. Stir in the reserved seeds.

Pour into sterilized jars (see page 98), cover each with a waxed paper disc and seal with the lids, then leave to cool and store in the refrigerator.

MAKES: 2 x 250 g (8 oz) jars
Preparation time: 5 minutes
Cooking time: 10 minutes (High pressure)

LEMON AND LIME CURD

3 eggs
1 unwaxed lemon
2 limes
200 g (7 oz) caster sugar
100 g (3½ oz) unsalted butter, cubed

There's no need to spend time stirring constantly, just make this delicious curd in your pressure cooker.

Beat the eggs together in a heatproof bowl. Finely grate the zest from the lemon and limes into the bowl, then squeeze in the juice, removing the pips.

Stir in the sugar, then add the butter. Loosely cover the bowl with nonstick baking paper. Place the trivet in the pressure cooker, pour in enough water so it doesn't touch the base of the bowl and place the bowl on the trivet.

Lock the lid, bring up to high pressure, stabilize the heat and cook for 10 minutes. Remove from the heat and slow release.

Carefully remove the bowl, then whisk vigorously until the butter is incorporated.

Pour into sterilized jars (see page 98) and seal with the lids, then store in the refrigerator. It will keep for up to 1 month in the refrigerator and for up to 1 month after opening.

MAKES: 4 x 450 g (14½ oz) jars
Preparation time: 15 minutes
Cooking time: about 35–45 minutes (High pressure),
   plus cooling and settling

EASY SEVILLE ORANGE MARMALADE

500 g (1 lb) whole Seville oranges
1 litre (1¾ pints) water
juice of 1 lemon
1 kg (2 lb) preserving sugar

Make this marmalade when Seville oranges are in season from mid-January. The unopened jars can be stored for up to a year.

Place the whole oranges in the pressure cooker. Pour over the measured water. Lock the lid, bring up to high pressure, stabilize the heat and cook for 15 minutes. Remove from the heat and slow release. The oranges will be soft.

Remove the oranges with a slotted spoon, leaving the liquid in the pressure cooker. When the oranges are cool enough to handle, cut them in half over a large bowl, then using a spoon, scoop out the inside pips and pith. Place the oranges back in the pressure cooker with any juice that has collected in the bowl. Lock the lid, bring back up to high pressure, stabilize the heat and cook for 5 minutes. Remove from the heat and slow release.

Strain the oranges through a sieve into a large bowl, pressing the pulp through with the back of a wooden spoon to extract the maximum amount of juice and pectin. Return to the cooker. Stir in the lemon juice and sugar. Cut the orange peel into thin or chunky shreds and add to the cooker.

Cook over a low heat, stirring until all of the sugar has dissolved, then boil for 15–20 minutes, stirring occasionally, until a little of the mixture dropped on to a chilled plate sets and wrinkles when you push your finger through it or the marmalade reaches a setting point of 105°C (221°F) on a sugar thermometer. Leave to settle for 15 minutes, then pour into sterilized jars (see page 98) and seal with the lids. Store the unopened jars in a cool, dark place.

SOMETHING SWEET

SERVES: 8
Preparation time: 15 minutes, plus chilling
Cooking time: 15 minutes (High pressure)

SALTED CARAMEL CHEESECAKE

**50 g (2 oz) unsalted butter, plus extra
for greasing**
**200 g (7 oz) plain chocolate digestive
biscuits, crushed**
chocolate curls, to decorate

For the filling:
400 g (13 oz) cream cheese
100 g (3½ oz) golden caster sugar
**200 g (8 oz) jar salted caramel sauce,
plus extra to serve (optional)**
100 ml (3½ fl oz) soured cream
1 teaspoon vanilla extract
3 eggs

Lightly grease a 20 cm (8 inch) loose-bottomed deep cake tin and line the base with nonstick baking paper. Melt the butter in a saucepan, then stir in the crushed biscuits. Press evenly into the base of the tin. Chill in the refrigerator while you make the filling.

Place the cream cheese, sugar and 200 g (7 oz) of the caramel sauce in a bowl and whisk together until smooth. Whisk in the soured cream, vanilla and eggs, then pour over the biscuit base.

Place the trivet or upturned steamer basket in the pressure cooker and pour in enough water to come just below the top of the trivet or basket. Make a foil handle by folding over a piece of foil to fit under the tin, then place the tin on the trivet or basket. Fold down the edges of the handle so they do not go over the top of the cheesecake. Alternatively, use a tea towel.

Lock the lid, bring up to high pressure, stabilize the heat and cook for 15 minutes. Remove from the heat and slow release.

Carefully remove the tin from the cooker using the foil handle or tea towel. Leave to cool at room temperature, then chill in the refrigerator for at least 4 hours, or overnight.

Top with chocolate curls and serve in slices with extra warm caramel sauce, if liked.

SERVES: 4
Preparation time: 20 minutes
Cooking time: 15 minutes (High pressure)

CITRUS SURPRISE PUDDING

50 g (2 oz) softened butter, plus extra
    for greasing
100 g (3½ oz) caster sugar
grated zest and juice of 1 small orange
grated zest and juice of 1 lemon
grated zest and juice of 1 lime
2 eggs, separated
50 g (2 oz) self-raising flour
175 ml (6 fl oz) milk
cream, to serve (optional)

This pudding separates on cooking, leaving a light sponge on top and a delicious citrus curd on the bottom.

Lightly grease a 20 cm (8 inch) round ovenproof dish or 1 litre (1¾ pint) soufflé dish.

Place the butter, sugar and zests of the fruits in a separate bowl and cream together with a hand-held whisk until fluffy. Beat in the egg yolks a little at a time. Fold in the flour, alternating it with the combined citrus juices, then stir in the milk.

Whisk the egg whites in a clean bowl until they form stiff peaks, then gently fold into the citrusy mixture. Pour into the prepared dish, cover the top with a piece of nonstick baking paper, so it does not touch the top of the pudding, secure with kitchen string, then cover with foil.

Place the trivet or upturned steamer basket in the pressure cooker, add the dish then pour in enough water to come just below the trivet or basket. Lock the lid, bring up to high pressure, stabilize the heat and cook for 15 minutes. Remove from the heat and slow release.

Carefully remove the dish from the cooker and then serve the pudding with cream, if liked.

SERVES: 10
Preparation time: 20 minutes
Cooking time: about 2 hours (High pressure)

ORANGE AND STEM GINGER CHRISTMAS PUDDING

softened butter, for greasing
400 g (134 oz) dried mixed fruit
50 g (2 oz) candied orange peel
50 g (2 oz) blanched almonds, chopped
grated zest and juice of 1 orange
1 teaspoon ground mixed spice
75 g (3 oz) self-raising flour
150 g (5 oz) shredded beef or vegetable suet
75 g (3 oz) fresh breadcrumbs
150 g (5 oz) soft dark brown sugar
4 pieces of stem ginger from a jar, chopped, plus 2 tablespoons ginger syrup from the jar
2 eggs
1 tablespoon black treacle
2 tablespoons orange-flavoured liqueur or brandy
75 ml (3 fl oz) milk
1 litre (1¾ pints) boiling water
brandy cream or butter, to serve

Thoroughly grease a 1.2 litre (2 pint) pudding basin. Stir all the dry ingredients together, with the stem ginger pieces in a large bowl. Beat the eggs, treacle, orange juice, ginger syrup and liqueur or brandy together in another bowl, then mix into the dry ingredients. Stir in the milk.

Spoon the mixture into the prepared pudding basin, pressing it down with the back of a spoon. Cut a round of greaseproof paper to fit the top, then cover with a piece of pleated foil. Secure with kitchen string, which can also make a handle.

Place the trivet in the pressure cooker, add the pudding, then pour in the measured water. Close the lid but do not lock it and steam naturally for 15 minutes. Lock the lid, bring up to high pressure, stabilize the heat and cook for 1 hour 45 minutes. Remove from the heat and slow release.

Remove carefully from the cooker, leave to cool, then store in a cool, dark place. To reheat, cook on high pressure for 15 minutes. Serve with brandy cream or butter.

SERVES: 6
Preparation time: 10 minutes, plus infusing and chilling
Cooking time: 15 minutes (High pressure)

LEMON GRASS AND CARDAMOM WHITE CHOCOLATE POTS

200 ml (7 fl oz) milk
300 ml (½ pint) single cream
25 g (1 oz) caster sugar
2 lemon grass stalks, tough outer layers removed and roughly chopped
4 green cardamom pods, seeds crushed
1 kaffir lime leaf, shredded
200 g (7 oz) good-quality white chocolate, broken into small pieces
5 egg yolks
white chocolate curls, to decorate

Place the milk, cream and sugar in a small saucepan, then add the lemon grass, cardamom seeds and kaffir lime leaf. Bring to the boil, then remove from the heat and leave to infuse for 20 minutes.

Place the chocolate in a heatproof bowl. Rewarm the infused cream, then pour the mixture through a sieve over the chocolate and stir until the chocolate has melted. Beat in the egg yolks.

Divide the mixture between 6 x 150 ml (¼ pint) small ramekins. Place the upturned steamer basket in the pressure cooker, add 3 of the ramekins, then pour in enough water to come just below the top of the basket. Lock the lid, bring up to high pressure, stabilize the heat and cook for 5 minutes. Remove from the heat and quick release.

Repeat with the remaining ramekins. Chill the pots in the refrigerator for at least 2 hours, then serve decorated with white chocolate curls.

SERVES: 4
Preparation time: 10 minutes
Cooking time: 35 minutes (High pressure)

STEAMED JAM ROLY-POLY

150 g (5 oz) self-raising flour , plus extra for dusting
pinch of salt
75 g (2 oz) shredded beef or vegetable suet
100–125 ml (3½–4 fl oz) cold water
200 g (7 oz) thick jam, plus extra to serve (optional)
custard, to serve

Mix the flour, salt and suet together in a large bowl, then stir in enough of the measured water to make a firm dough. Roll the dough out on a work surface lightly dusted with flour to a rectangle about 15 x 30 cm (6 x 12 inches).

Spread the dough thickly with the jam, leaving a 1 cm (½ inch) border. Brush the edges with a little water and roll up tightly from a short end. Wrap loosely in nonstick baking paper, then in foil, crimping the ends.

Place the upturned steamer basket or trivet in the pressure cooker and add the roly-poly. Pour in enough boiling water to come just below the top of the trivet or basket. Close the lid but do not lock it and steam naturally for 10 minutes. Lock the lid, bring up to high pressure, stabilize the heat and cook for 25 minutes. Remove from the heat and slow release.

Carefully remove the roly-poly, then upwrap and serve in thick slices with custard and extra jam, if liked.

SERVES: 6
Preparation time: 10 minutes
Cooking time: 15 minutes (High pressure)

SELF-SAUCING STICKY TOFFEE PUDDING

50 g (2 oz) butter, melted and cooled, plus extra for greasing
125g (4 oz) dried pitted dates, chopped
½ teaspoon bicarbonate of soda
100 ml (3½ fl oz) boiling water
75 g (3 oz) dark muscovado sugar
125g (4 oz) self-raising flour
100 ml (3½ fl oz) evaporated or full-fat milk
1 egg
1 teaspoon vanilla extract
vanilla ice cream, to serve

For the sauce:
150 g (5 oz) dark muscovado sugar
25 g (1 oz) butter, cubed
400 ml (14 fl oz) boiling water

Grease a 20 cm (8 inch), 1 litre (1¾ pint) round soufflé dish. Place the dates in a heatproof bowl, sprinkle with the bicarbonate of soda and pour over the 100 ml (3½ fl oz) water. Leave to soften while you make the pudding.

Place the sugar and flour in a bowl and mix together. Whisk the milk, egg, vanilla and melted butter together in a jug, then stir into the flour mixture. Mash the dates roughly with the back of a fork, then fold into the mixture.

Spoon the mixture into the prepared dish, spoon over the sugar for the sauce, dot with the butter, then carefully pour over the measured water. Cover loosely with nonstick baking paper, so it doesn't touch the pudding, then cover with foil.

Place the trivet or upturned steamer basket in the pressure cooker and pour in enough water to come just below the top of the trivet or basket. Carefully lower in the dish then lock the lid, bring up to high pressure, stabilize the heat and cook for 15 minutes. Remove from the heat and slow release. Serve hot with vanilla ice cream.

SERVES: 8–10
Preparation time: 10 minutes
Cooking time: 10 minutes (High pressure)

SEA SALT CHOCOLATE FUDGE BROWNIES

125 g (4 oz) butter, plus extra for greasing

150 g (5 oz) plain dark chocolate chips or plain dark chocolate, broken into small pieces (at least 70% cocoa solids)

200 g (7 oz) golden caster sugar

2 large eggs

1 teaspoon vanilla extract

100 g (3½ oz) plain flour

25 g (1 oz) cocoa powder, sifted

½ teaspoon baking powder

1 teaspoon sea salt

These chocolate brownies are deliciously fudgy. Omit the sea salt and try adding some chopped nuts or white chocolate chips for variations, if liked.

Grease an 18 cm (7 inch) and line the base of the cake tin with nonstick baking paper.

Melt the butter and chocolate in a heatproof bowl set over a saucepan of simmering water, stirring occasionally. Make sure the bottom of the bowl doesn't touch the water. Remove from the heat and leave to cool slightly.

Beat the sugar, eggs and vanilla together in a large bowl with a hand-held whisk until pale and fluffy.

Whisk in the chocolate mixture until well combined, then, using a metal spoon, stir in the flour, cocoa powder, baking powder and salt.

Pour the mixture into the prepared tin. Place the trivet or upturned steamer basket in the pressure cooker, add the tin, then pour in enough water, to come just below the top of the trivet or basket. Lock the lid, bring up to high pressure, stabilize the heat and cook for 10 minutes. Remove from the heat and slow release.

Carefully remove the tin. The brownies will be just set and the centre will be slightly gooey. Leave to cool in the tin for 10 minutes, then transfer to a wire rack.

When completely cold, remove the baking paper and cut the brownies into squares. They are also delicious served in wedges while slightly warm with ice cream.

SERVES: 8–10
Preparation time: 20 minutes, plus chilling
Cooking time: 5 minutes (High pressure)

CHOCOLATE ORANGE MOUSSE CAKE

150 g (5 oz) unsalted butter, plus extra
    for greasing
300 g (10 oz) good-quality plain dark
    chocolate with orange (70% cocoa
    solids), broken into pieces
6 eggs, separated
125 g (4 oz) caster sugar

To serve:
300 ml (½ pint) double cream
zest of 1 orange, finely grated or in
    strips
cocoa powder, for dusting

You can vary the flavour by using different-flavoured chocolate, such as chilli, mint or coconut – just remember to keep the cocoa solids content to 70%.

Lightly grease a 20 cm (8 inch) cake tin, (8 cm/3½ inches deep) and line the base with nonstick baking paper. Melt the chocolate and butter in a heatproof bowl set over a saucepan of simmering water. Make sure the bottom of the bowl doesn't touch the water.

Meanwhile, place the egg yolks in a bowl with the sugar and whisk together with a hand-held electric whisk until very thick and pale. Stir in the melted chocolate mixture.

Whisk the egg whites in a large clean bowl until they form soft peaks. Fold 2 tablespoons of the egg whites into the chocolate mixture to loosen it slightly, then using a large metal spoon, gently fold in the remaining egg whites.

Pour the mixture into the prepared tin. Place the trivet or unturned steamer basket in the pressure cooker and pour in enough water to come just below the top of the trivet or basket. Make a foil handle by folding over a piece of foil to fit under the tin, then place the tin on the trivet or basket. Fold down the edges of the handle so they do not go over the top of the cake. Alternatively, use a tea towel.

Lock the lid, bring up to high pressure, stabilize the heat and cook for 5 minutes. Remove from the heat and slow release.

Remove the tin from the cooker and leave to cool at room temperature, then chill in the refrigerator for 2 hours.

Remove the cake from the refrigerator 30 minutes before you want to serve. Whip the cream until it forms soft peaks, then serve in slices with a dollop of the cream, decorated with orange zest and a dusting of cocoa powder.

SERVES: 4
Preparation time: 5 minutes
Cooking time: about 13 minutes (Low pressure)

VANILLA-POACHED PEARS WITH WARM FUDGE SAUCE

150 g (5 oz) light soft brown sugar
1 vanilla pod, halved lengthways and seeds scraped out or 1 teaspoon vanilla bean paste
1 tablespoon lemon juice
125 ml (4 fl oz) water
4 firm pears, peeled, halved and cored
100 g (3½ oz) unsalted butter
150 ml (¼ pint) double cream
1 tablespoon golden syrup
vanilla ice cream, to serve (optional)

These pears are very quick to cook so are perfect for entertaining.

Place 50 g (2 oz) of the sugar, the vanilla pod and seeds or bean paste, lemon juice and measured water in the pressure cooker. Bring to a simmer, stirring constantly until the sugar has dissolved.

Add the pears. Lock the lid, bring up to low pressure, stabilize the heat and cook for 3 minutes. Remove from the heat and quick release.

Transfer the pears to warmed plates, add the butter, remaining sugar, cream and syrup to the cooker and cook gently over a low heat for 2–3 minutes until the butter has melted. Gently bring to the boil, stirring constantly, for 4–5 minutes until the sauce thickens slightly. Remove from the heat.

Pour the fudge sauce over the top of the pears and serve immediately with a scoop of vanilla ice cream, if liked.

SERVES: 4
Preparation time: 10 minutes, plus cooling
Cooking time: about 5 minutes (Low pressure)

POACHED PEACHES WITH POMEGRANATE AND ROSEWATER SYRUP

1 tablespoon pomegranate molasses
25 g (1 oz) caster sugar
1–2 teaspoons rosewater, or to taste
400 ml (14 fl oz) water
4 firm peaches, halved and stoned

To serve:
handful of pistachio kernels, chopped
pomegranate seeds
edible dried rose petals (optional)

Use firm peaches, otherwise they will become too soft.

Place the pomegranate molasses, sugar, 1 teaspoon of the rosewater and measured water in the pressure cooker over a medium heat, stirring constantly until the sugar has dissolved. Taste and add more rosewater, if liked.

Add the peach halves. Lock the lid, bring up to low pressure, stabilize the heat and cook for 1 minute. Remove from the heat and quick release.

Transfer the peaches to a bowl. Taste the syrup and add a little more rosewater, if liked, then boil the syrup to reduce if necessary. Pour the syrup over the peaches.

Leave the peaches to cool and infuse. Serve 2 peach halves in a bowl, then pour over some of the syrup. Sprinkle over the pistachio nuts, pomegranate seeds and a few dried rose petals, if using.

SERVES: 4–6
Preparation time: 10 minutes
Cooking time: 50 minutes (High pressure)

STEAMED SYRUP PUDDING

150 g (5 oz) softened butter, plus extra for greasing
4 tablespoons golden syrup, plus extra to serve
1 tablespoon white breadcrumbs
150 g (5 oz) golden caster sugar
finely grated zest of 1 lemon
2 large eggs, beaten
150 g (5 oz) self-raising flour
2 tablespoons milk
custard or cream, to serve

Heavily grease a 1 litre (1¾ pint) pudding basin. Pour in the golden syrup, then stir in the breadcrumbs.

Cream the butter, sugar and lemon zest together in a bowl using a hand-held whisk until light and fluffy. Gradually beat in the eggs, then fold in the flour and milk.

Spoon the mixture into the prepared pudding basin and cover with a circle of nonstick baking paper, then cover with a piece of pleated foil, so the pudding can rise.

Place the trivet or upturned steamer basket in the pressure cooker, add the pudding, then pour in enough boiling water to come just below the top of the trivet.

Close the lid but do not lock it and steam naturally for 15 minutes. Lock the lid, bring up to high pressure, stabilize the heat and cook for 35 minutes. Remove from the heat and slow release.

Carefully remove the pudding and turn out on to a serving plate. Spoon over a little extra syrup and serve with custard or cream.

SERVES: 4
Preparation time: 5 minutes
Cooking time: 12 minutes (High pressure)

CREAMY VANILLA RICE PUDDING

100 g (3½ oz) short-grain pudding rice
50 g (2 oz) caster sugar
400 ml (14 fl oz) can evaporated milk
200 ml (7 fl oz) water
1 vanilla pod, split lengthways
jam of your choice, to serve (optional)

You can transfer the rice pudding to a heated ovenproof dish and grill until you have some brown spots, if you like a skin on it.

Place all the ingredients except the jam in the pressure cooker. Lock the lid, bring up to high pressure, stabilize the heat and cook for 12 minutes. Remove from the heat and slow release.

Stir well, then cover with the lid and leave to stand for 2–3 minutes. The rice will continue to cook and the mixture thicken. Remove the vanilla pod.

Serve in bowls with a dollop of jam, if liked.

SERVES: 8
Preparation time: 10 minutes, plus chilling overnight
Cooking time: about 45 minutes (Low pressure)

CRÈME CARAMEL

For the caramel:
175 g (6 oz) golden caster sugar
2 tablespoons warm water

For the custard:
300 ml (½ pint) milk
300 ml (½ pint) double cream
3 eggs
2 egg yolks
50 g (2 oz) caster sugar
1 teaspoon vanilla extract

First, make the caramel. Place the sugar in a heavy saucepan and place over a medium heat. Leave it, without stirring, until the sugar begins to melt and turns into liquid all around the edges. Don't be tempted to stir it.

Give the pan a good shake, the leave it over the heat until about one-quarter of the sugar has melted. Using a wooden spoon, stir the mixture gently until the sugar crystals have all transformed into liquid. Continue to cook, stirring occasionally, until it is a dark caramel colour.

Remove from the heat and add the measured water. Stand back as it may splutter a bit at this stage. Return the pan to a low heat and stir to melt any lumps that may form. Now quickly pour it into a 1.25 litre (2 pint) soufflé dish or 16 cm (6¼ inch) round ovenproof dish, about 16 cm (6¼ inches) in diameter, swirling it around to coat the bottom and up the sides a little.

Meanwhile, pour the milk and cream into another pan and leave it to heat gently while you whisk the eggs, egg yolks, sugar and vanilla together in a large bowl. When the milk mixture is hot, pour it on to the egg and sugar mixture, whisking until it is thoroughly blended. Pour the liquid through a sieve into the soufflé dish or ovenproof dish and cover tightly with foil.

Place the trivet or upturned steamer basket in the pressure cooker and pour in enough water to come just below the top of the trivet or basket. Carefully lower in the dish.

Lock the lid, bring up to low pressure, stabilize the heat and cook for 30 minutes. Remove from the heat and slow release. Remove the dish from the cooker, cool at room temperature for 15 minutes, then chill in the refrigerator overnight.

When ready to serve, gently ease the pudding from the edges of the dish and carefully invert on to a plate.

SERVES: 12
Preparation time: 5 minutes, plus cooling
Cooking time: 25 minutes (High pressure)

TROPICAL FRUIT CAKE

125 g (4 oz) unsalted butter, cubed, plus extra for greasing

100 g (3½ oz) raisins or sultanas

250 g (8 oz) soft mixed dried tropical fruit such as pineapple, mango, papaya, apricots, cut into small pieces, plus extra pieces for the topping

1 teaspoon ground mixed spice

2 teaspoons ground ginger

125 g (4 oz) soft brown light sugar

150 ml (¼ pint) cold water

225 g (7½ oz) self-raising flour

1 egg, beaten

Substitute the mixed tropical fruit with a mixture of currants, chopped dates, sultanas and glacé cherries for a traditional fruit cake.

Grease a 15 cm (6 inch) cake tin (about 7 cm/3 inches deep) and line the base with nonstick baking paper.

Place the raisins or sultanas, dried tropical fruit, mixed spice, ginger, butter, sugar and measured water in a medium saucepan. Warm over a low heat until the butter has melted, stirring occasionally with a wooden spoon, then bring to the boil. Boil the fruit for 5 minutes, then remove from the heat and leave to cool in the pan.

When the mixture is cool, stir in the flour and egg until well combined, then spoon into the prepared tin. Scatter a little dried fruit over the top.

Place the trivet or the upturned steamer basket in the pressure cooker, add the tin, then pour in enough water to come just below the top of the trivet or basket. Lock the lid, bring up to high pressure, stabilize the heat and cook for 15 minutes. Remove from the heat and slow release.

Remove the cake from the cooker and leave to cool in the tin. When cool, serve in slices. It will keep in and airtight container for up to 1 week.

INDEX

GLOSSARY

UK	US	UK	US	UK	US
aubergine	eggplant	chilli flakes	red pepper flakes	plain flour	all-purpose flour
back bacon	Canadian bacon	double cream	heavy cream	prawns	shrimp
baking paper	parchment paper	glacé cherries	candied cherries	pudding basin	ovenproof bowl
baking tray	rimmed baking sheet	greaseproof paper	waxed paper	rocket	arugula
bicarbonate of soda	baking soda	grill	broiler	self-raising flour	self-rising flour
black treacle	blackstrap molasses	golden syrup	light corn syrup	sieve	strainer
cake tin	cake pan	jug	pitcher	spring onions	scallions
caster sugar	superfine sugar	kitchen paper	paper towels	sultanas	golden raisins
coriander	cilantro	mangetout	snow peas	tea towel	dish towel
cornflour	cornstarch	natural yogurt	plain yogurt		
chestnut mushrooms	cremini mushrooms	passata	strained tomatoes		